IMPRESSIONS of home™
A PHOTO ESSAY OF HOMES & PLACES FOR REAL PEOPLE

EDITOR	Bruce Arant
WRITER	Joyce Brown
PLANS MANAGER	Tina Libe
GRAPHIC DESIGNERS	Jeff Dedlow
	Heather Guthrie
	Beverly Nelligan
	Annette Guy
ILLUSTRATOR	Heather Guthrie
RENDERING ILLUSTRATORS	Shawn Doherty
	Silvia Boyd
	Perry Gauthier
	George McDonald, dec.
TECHNICAL ADVISER	Carl Cuozzo
	Tom Clark
	Rob Phillips
CIRCULATION MANAGER	Priscilla Ivey
CO-PUBLISHERS	Dennis Brozak
	Linda Reimer

IMPRESSIONS of home™
A PHOTO ESSAY OF
HOMES & PLACES FOR REAL PEOPLE

IS PUBLISHED BY:
Design Basics Publications
11112 John Galt Blvd., Omaha, NE 68137
Web – www.designbasics.com
E-Mail – info@designbasics.com

CHIEF EXECUTIVE OFFICER	Dennis Brozak
PRESIDENT	Linda Reimer
DIRECTOR OF MARKETING	Kevin Blair
BUSINESS DEVELOPMENT	Paul Foresman
CONTROLLER	Janie Murnane
EDITOR-IN-CHIEF	Bruce Arant

Text and Design © 2002 by Design Basics Inc.
All rights reserved.

No part of this publication may be reproduced in any form or by any means without prior written permission of the publisher.

COVER PHOTO: Plan #44M-3096 Torrey
As seen on page 63
BUILDER: Blake Homes

LIBRARY OF CONGRESS NUMBER: 99-074748
ISBN: 1-892150-16-6

ONE-STORY HOME PLANS

PLAN #	PLAN NAME	SQ. FT.	PAGE #
2761	Mayberry	1341'	46
8013	Gabriel Bay	1392'	77
3010	Quimby	1422'	62
3019	Kelsey	1479'	17
2300	Adair	1496'	22
3127	Haley	1554'	9
2196	Granite	1561'	7
3578	Stonybrook	1595'	83
2290	Monterey	1666'	19
2212	Seville	1735'	19
24003	Tuxford	1762'	43
3577	Bennett	1782'	63
3587	Charleston	1796'	77
3006	Grayson	1806'	61
1559	Bancroft	1808'	53
2461	Shawnee	1850'	32
2799	Hawthorne	1887'	50
1748	Sinclair	1911'	69
2361	Summerwood	2015'	80
2222	Plainview	2068'	66
3597	Concorde	2132'	72
2326	Greensboro	2172'	39
3058	Montgomery	2311'	67
2652	Lawrence	2512'	24

1½-STORY HOME PLANS

PLAN #	PLAN NAME	SQ. FT.	PAGE #
3121	Bellamy	1660'	6
2245	Tyndale	1685'	67
8095	Sun Valley	1694'	79
8094	Angel Cove	1715'	31
5151	Sedona	1755'	18
2281	Ingram	1778'	29
8096	Pine Ridge	1837'	45
3063	Taylor	1957'	61
1380	Paterson	1999'	75
3381	Amanda	2037'	51
3064	Eldridge	2055'	62
2745	Sierra	2089'	64
2285	Prairie	2115'	56
24004	Bardel	2248'	73
1554	Chandler	2276'	13
2701	Ambrose	2340'	45
1862	Manchester	2353'	81
2203	Ashton	2391'	15
2261	Arant	2405'	55
2702	Ellison	2432'	71
2311	Pinehurst	2486'	41
2956	Briarwood	2562'	23
4081	Hanna	2576'	70
2309	Edmonton	2579'	29
2894	Rollins	2603'	60
4134	Schuyler	2613'	76

1½-STORY HOME PLANS

PLAN #	PLAN NAME	SQ. FT.	PAGE #
2723	Armburst	2645'	46
2460	Bridgeport	2695'	28
24015	Fairview	2755'	27
3494	Thornhill	2850'	35
2458	Hartford	2932'	8
2800	Appleton	2979'	47
4144	Marlow	3040'	83
2322	Northland	3067'	42
9162	Tealwood Estate	3072'	38
2249	Normandy	3172'	49
2475	Winchester	3556'	40
9143	Oak Grove Estate	3750'	11
2733	Fairchild	3904'	33
9114	Meadowview Manor	4139'	59

TWO-STORY HOME PLANS

PLAN #	PLAN NAME	SQ. FT.	PAGE #
8108	Rose Hollow	1705'	57
2890	Jefferson	1732'	26
3096	Torrey	1768'	63
3581	Paige	1771'	76
1868	Somerset	1842'	14
2100	Fenton	1845'	58
2235	Albany	1931'	28
2315	Harrisburg	1993'	5
2619	Oakbrook	1998'	51
2401	Curtiss	2058'	31
1870	Bristol	2078'	16
8072	Hamilton Farm	2095'	78
2638	Linden	2103'	14
2618	Paisley	2131'	44
4952	Caldera	2144'	54
2408	Crawford	2270'	35
1771	McGregor	2279'	13
8011	Jones Farm	2292'	82
8052	Norris Crossing	2303'	25
1856	Derby	2327'	47
2414	Stanton	2343'	44
4135	Gerard	2349'	78
2919	Fulton	2412'	10
5086	Patagonia	2417'	21
2346	Fayette	2480'	30
2650	Norwick	2481'	60
1455	Newberry	2594'	65
9161	Woodvine Manor	2715'	34
2746	Winrock	2775'	30
2374	Rothschild	2870'	79
2207	Manning	2914'	74
987	Santa Ana	3025'	12
2294	Princeton	3031'	12
2043	Gainsborough	3235'	15
3156	Jacksonville	3273'	37
2332	Corinth	3775'	48

A Photo Essay of
Homes & Places for Real People

Where are you from?

It is a question frequently asked because it reveals so much about who we are. The place we live gives us our sense of roots. Some of us choose to live in the same area we grew up in. Others end up living in many different areas throughout our lives. If we're lucky, we feel we belong wherever we wind up.

The place we live molds our identity.
The way we speak, dress and look at things are affected by the region we live in. Seasonal weather patterns determine many of our activities. The ethnic mix in our area influences our culture– the styles of art and music we enjoy and the traditions and customs we keep.

Our tastes also adapt to regional cuisine:
New England clam bakes and Boston baked beans… expresso and cappuccino… jambalaya… biscuits and gravy… blackeyed peas… chile rellenos… crispy polenta… bratwurst… Swedish meatballs… and corn-fed roast beef.

The question "Where are you from?" triggers widely differing images, depending on the part of the country you call home: A lonely saguaro cactus standing guard over shifting sands beneath a cloudless sky. A massive oak tree draped in a moss-fringed shawl on the grounds of an old

plantation. A towering windmill silhouetted by a prairie sunset. A quaint, covered bridge spanning a peaceful river in New England. Tree-covered mountains rising from chilly, Northwestern waters.

IMPRESSIONS of home™ - A Photo Essay of Homes & Places for Real People, presents one-hundred home designs which have been built all across America, demonstrating their adaptability to any locale. But as you'll see, this is more than just a book of house plans. Because homes are about the people who live in them, we've included real peoples' impressions on living in these homes and life in their area. Additionally, throughout the following pages, photographs and reflections on life in different regions will take you on a brief journey to sample the rich diversity and the unique flavors which make up this great country.

Along the journey, all of us at Design Basics hope you'll find the ideal plan in IMPRESSIONS of home™ – no matter where you choose to live.

NEW ENGLAND

Like Americana art that's come to life— settings that seem too perfect to be real: A green lace canopy over a winding dirt road. A scarecrow guarding mounds of pumpkins. Quaint town squares nestled in the woods. Red farm houses and white steepled churches. Old stone fences. Picturesque fishing villages in hidden harbors. Hills ablaze in a riot of yellow, orange, and red. Evergreens covered with ice diamonds sparkling in the sunlight.

A cultural corner. Home to Yale, Harvard, and MIT... world-class museums, art galleries, and orchestras... Norman Rockwell and well-known literary figures (Ralph W. Emerson, Emily Dickinson, Robert Frost, and Dr. Seuss, to name a few). A land rich in history where men like Roger Williams, Paul Revere, Ethan Allen, and Benjamin Franklin forged a nation.

Where children float on inner-tubes in secluded swimming holes, Christmas carolers ride in horse-drawn sleighs, neighbors bring covered dishes when someone is ill, anyone can have his say in small town meetings, and visitors feel homesick for the quiet life even before they leave.

New Englanders are solid people who meet problems with a wry grin and a shrug and relish simple pleasures: Dangling a fishing line over the side of a canoe or down a hole drilled in the ice. Hunting deer, grouse, turkey, and moose. Mountain biking up and down rolling hills. Sailing, hiking, and camping. Pouring fresh maple syrup over a stack of fluffy pancakes. Sipping clam chowder beside a crackling fire. Sitting on a porch swing counting one's blessings.

IMPRESSIONS— Homes & Places for Real People

BUILT BY: The Wilson Family and Grandpa

A. Harrisburg

#44M-2315 *Price Code* 19

Main: 1000 SQ. FT.
Second: 993 SQ. FT.

Total: 1993 SQ. FT.

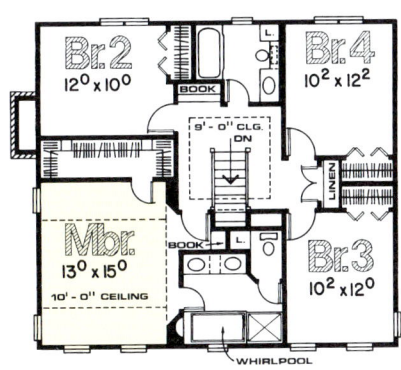

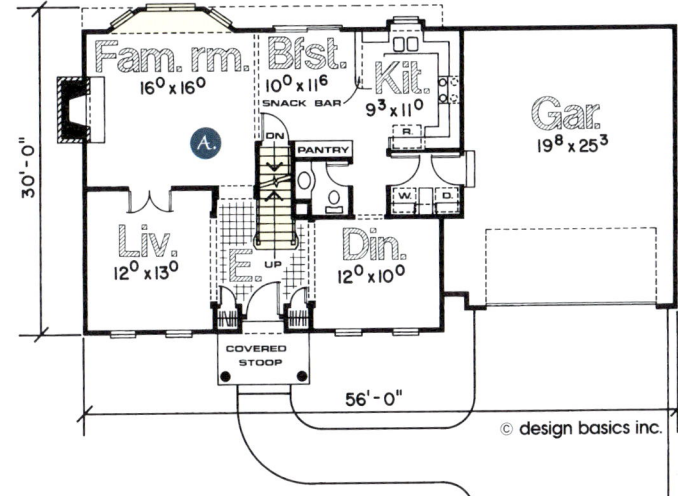

© design basics inc.

DESIGN QUALITY #1

A. THE HARRISBURG
B. THE BELLAMY
C. THE GRANITE

NEW ENGLAND SIMPLICITY...

You don't have to live in a tiny village in Vermont to long for the simple life. After all, some of the nicest things are the simplest: Meat loaf and mashed potatoes. A bowl of fresh popcorn and a rented movie. The smell of freshly mown grass. A sun-streaked sky after a rain. A moonlit walk. An impromptu picnic. A group of good friends playing cards. Children's laughter. By the same token, a home doesn't have to be elaborate to be perfectly lovely.

3 VIEWS...

A. From its smooth, classic exterior to its simple traffic flow and rectangular shaped rooms, the Harrisburg is a traditional colonial. An open staircase in the entry, bayed windows in the family room and sloped ceilings in the master bedroom add a few surprises.

B. Subtle design details enhance the Bellamy: a boxed ceiling in the master bedroom, a sloped ceiling in the dining room, transom-topped windows on either side of the fireplace in the great room and sunny, boxed windows in the breakfast area and kitchen.

C. Although the Granite's efficient floor plan wastes no space, it feels very roomy. The entry provides a view of the fireplace and raised hearth in the great room. Combining the dining and great rooms makes the area more flexible and appear bigger.

ORDER DIRECT - (800) 947-7526 www.designbasics.com

BUILT BY: Craftmaster Construction

B. Bellamy

#44M-3121 *Price Code* 16

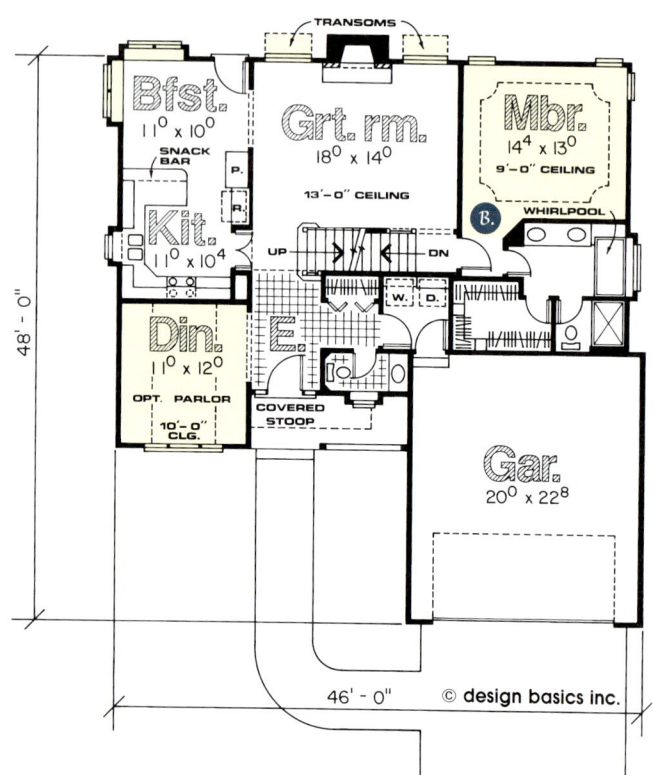
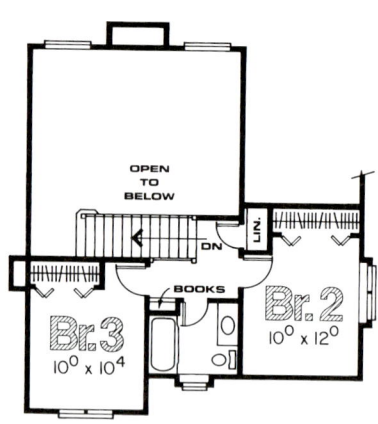

Main: 1265 Sq. Ft.
Second: 395 Sq. Ft.

Total: 1660 Sq. Ft.

IMPRESSIONS— Homes & Places for Real People

BUILT BY: MJ Schultz Builders

C. Granite

#44M-2196 *Price Code 15*

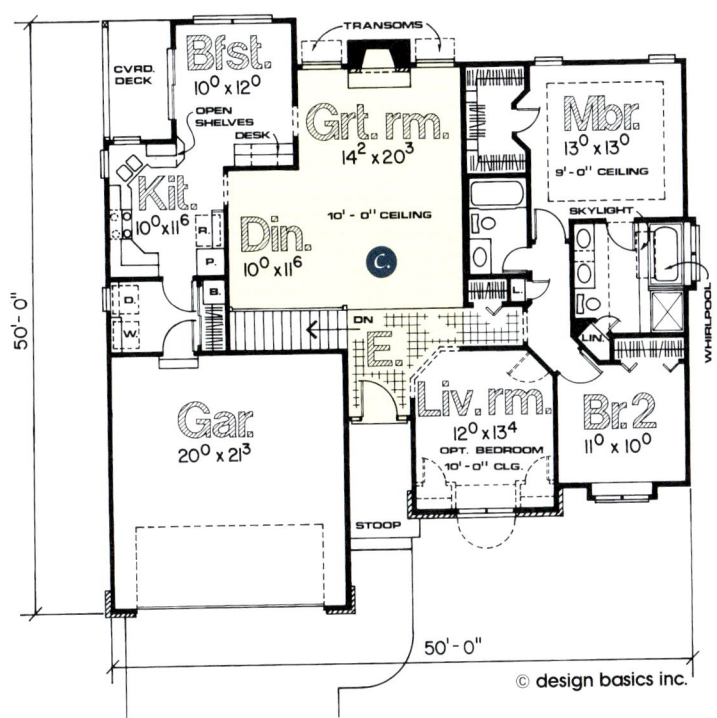

1561 Finished Sq. Ft.

ORDER DIRECT- (800) 947-7526 www.designbasics.com

Home Owner Impressions

on living in the Hartford

BUILT BY: Weinandy Construction

Hartford

#44M-2458 Price Code 29

Main: 2084 Sq. Ft.
Second: 848 Sq. Ft.

Total: 2932 Sq. Ft.

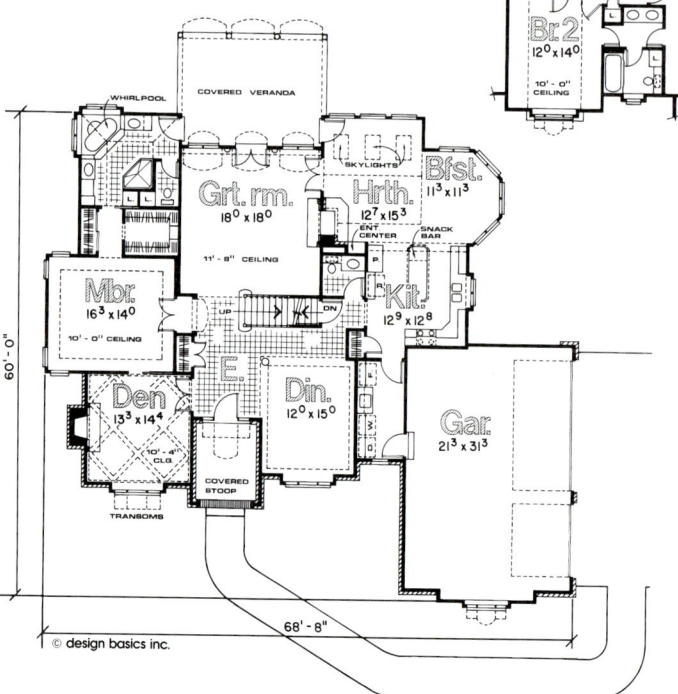

It wouldn't be unusual to see an acquaintance walk straight into Peter and Roxanne's home without knocking, call out a "Hello" and grab a refreshment out of the refrigerator. This unpretentious atmosphere is exactly what Peter and Roxanne strive for in their home, Design Basics' "Hartford."

"We enjoy having family and friends over and people taking advantage of the house," Peter states simply.

Though Peter and Roxanne live in the New England area, their home is a far cry from their previous Dutch Colonial home, a traditional style that dominates the landscape. "In this home, there are very few interior walls, whereas in our previous home, each area was an individual room. So if you were in the kitchen, you were closed off from the rest of the house," Peter says.

The Hartford's floor plan suits Peter, Roxanne and their two son's lifestyle ideally. It does so because they didn't try to stick to the confines of the home's intended room arrangements. For example, they use the den– located just inside the entry– as a combination music and reading room where their son frequently practices on their grand piano.

"It's worked out very well," Roxanne says. "If our son is

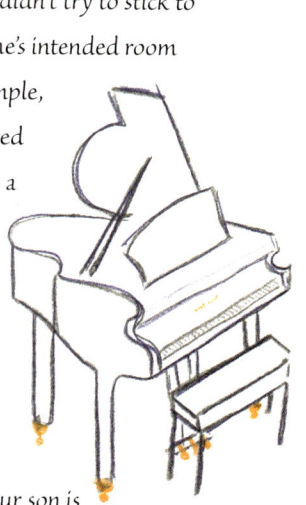

continued on page 10

IMPRESSIONS – *Homes & Places for Real People*

BUILT BY: Bilstad Building, Inc.

Fulton

#44M- 2919   Price Code 24

practicing for any length of time, we just close the French doors. He can concentrate and life in the rest of the house goes on."

The bayed area in the kitchen, designated as an informal eating area, is used as a homework and computer area. Roxanne, who is finishing the last year of an English degree, and her two sons use the area to study, write papers and prepare for class. "Because it's central to the house, you're not removed from the rest of the family when you're doing your work. And there are so many windows that it makes the area a beautiful place to be," Roxanne says.

The hearth room, with a cathedral ceiling and three lovely skylights, is where the family eats on a daily basis.

It's no doubt that their house was a perfect fit, but moving from a well-established neighborhood to one where they were the third house on the street was a different story. Although they'd lived in New England all of their lives, they felt like they were starting over in many ways.

They demonstrated their love of entertaining just three weeks after they moved in by hosting a party for their new neighbors. Soon food drives and pool parties became regular events. The group even created a tongue-in-cheek neighborhood association to "sponsor" their many get-togethers.

"I think all of the people on our street would say that when you turn down our street, it feels like our own little piece of the world. We all look out for each other," Roxanne says.

And whether it's to stop and visit or just to say a quick "Hello," the folks who live on Peter and Roxanne's street know there's one place they're always welcome.

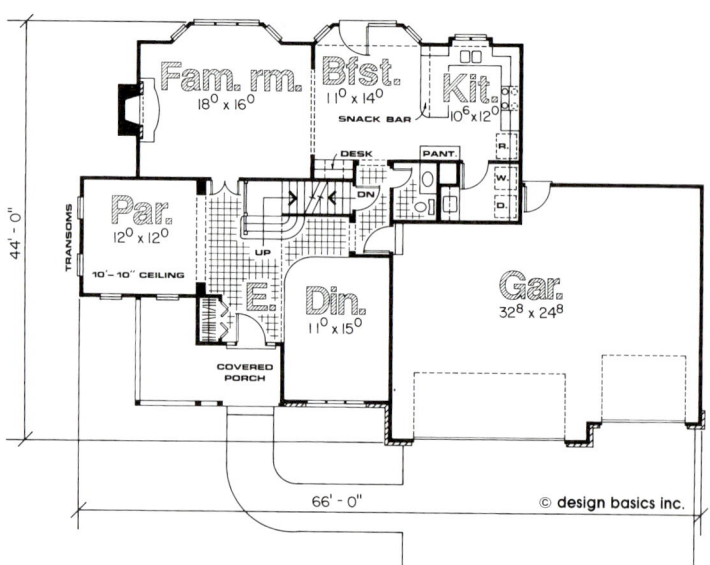

Main: 1277 Sq. Ft.
Second: 1135 Sq. Ft.

Total: 2412 Sq. Ft.

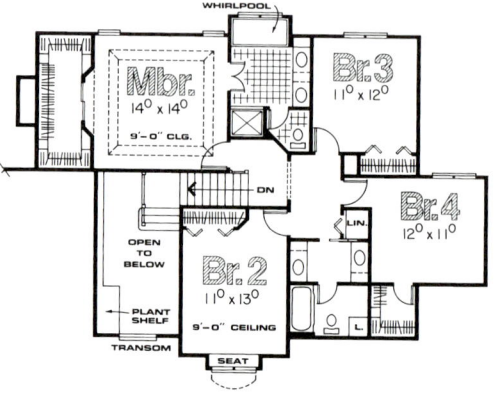

IMPRESSIONS– *Homes & Places for Real People*

BUILT BY: Golba Construction

Oak Grove Estate

#44M-9143 *Price Code 37*

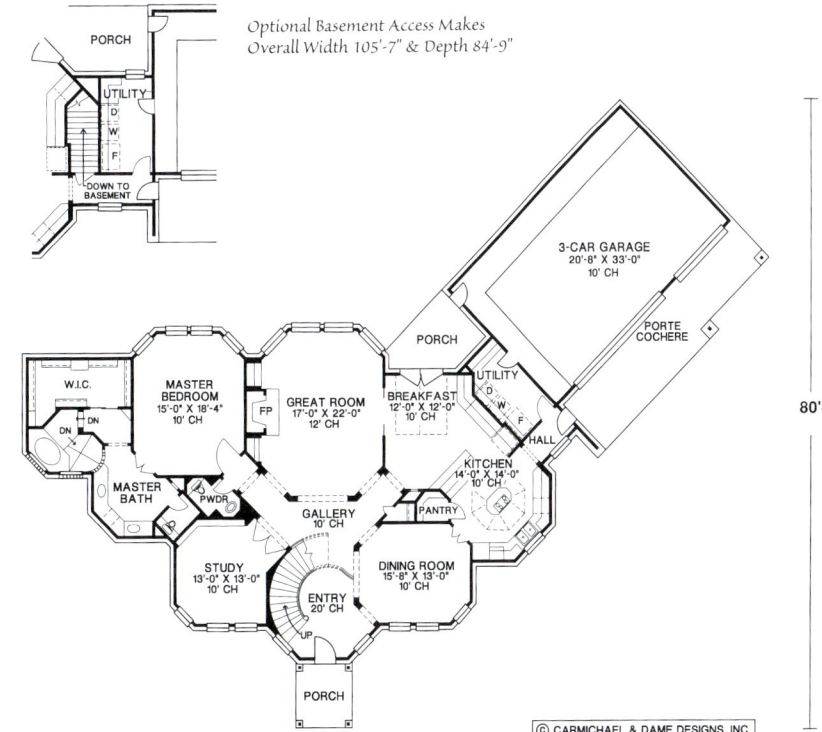

Optional Basement Access Makes
Overall Width 105'-7" & Depth 84'-9"

Main: 2274 Sq. Ft.
Second: 1476 Sq. Ft.

Total: 3750 Sq. Ft.

NOTE: 9 ft. main level walls

ORDER DIRECT - (800) 947-7526   www.designbasics.com

This home may have been altered from the plan's original design.

BUILT BY: Bilstad Building, Inc.

#44M-987   *Price Code 30*

Santa Ana

BUILT BY: Quality First Construction

Princeton

#44M-2294   *Price Code 30*

Kitchen/breakfast area features bayed window, wrapping counter, built-in hutch and desk, pantry and extra large island snack bar.

Roomy laundry provides clothes rod, soaking sink and space for a freezer.

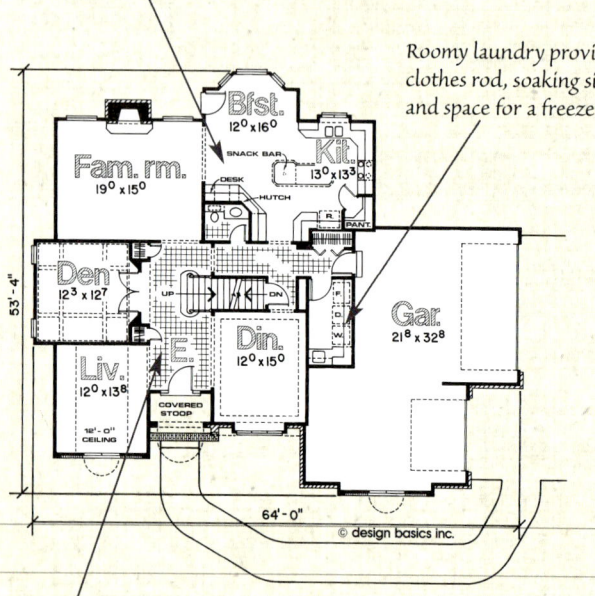

This home may have been altered from the plan's original design.

A sunken family room with spider-beamed ceiling, has a bayed window, wet bar and see-thru fireplace.

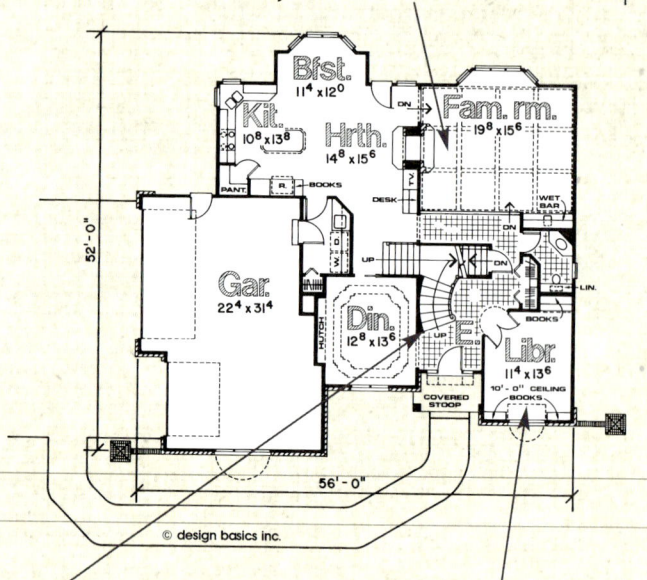

Two-story entry with boxed ceiling, sidelights and an arched transom above the door offers a view into the formal living and dining rooms.

Two-story entry with lovely, curved staircase offers view of dining room with striking ceiling detail.

Library has 10-foot-high ceiling, large window with arched transom, three bookcases and French doors.

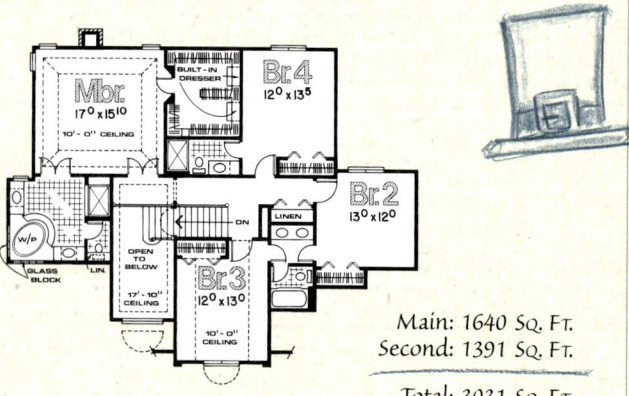

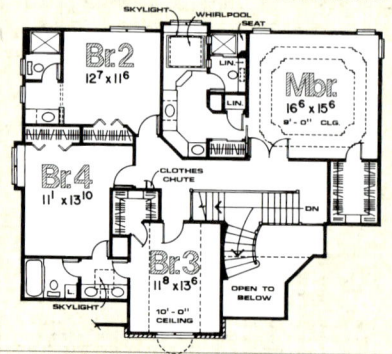

Main: 1640 SQ. FT.
Second: 1391 SQ. FT.

Total: 3031 SQ. FT.

Main: 1583 SQ. FT.
Second: 1442 SQ. FT.

Total: 3025 SQ. FT.

12

IMPRESSIONS— *Homes & Places for Real People*

This home may have been altered from the plan's original design.

BUILT BY: Tweedt Engineering & Construction

McGregor

#44M-1771   *Price Code 22*

BUILT BY: Tweedt Engineering & Construction

Chandler

#44M-1554   *Price Code 22*

A vaulted ceiling and corner windows add luster to the master bedroom.

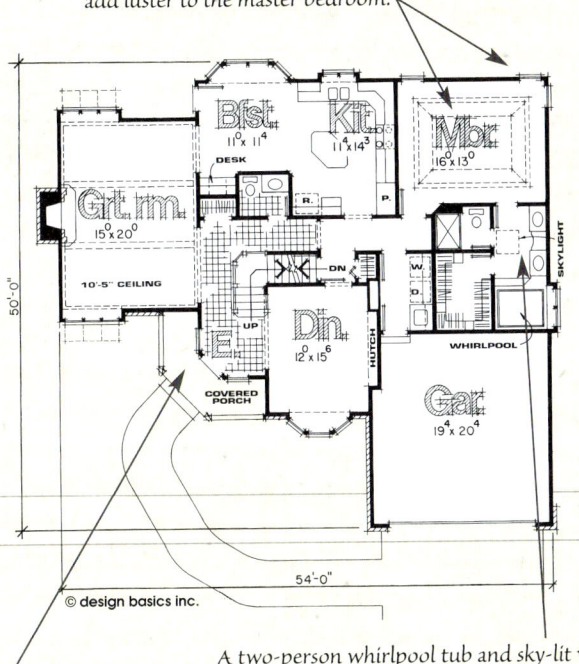

A two-person whirlpool tub and sky-lit vanity give a romantic air to the master bath.

The angle of the front porch adds beauty to the home's exterior curb appeal.

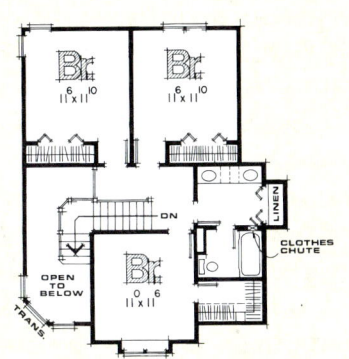

Main: 1551 SQ. FT.
Second: 725 SQ. FT.
Total: 2276 SQ. FT.

See-thru fireplace enhances both the living room and family room.

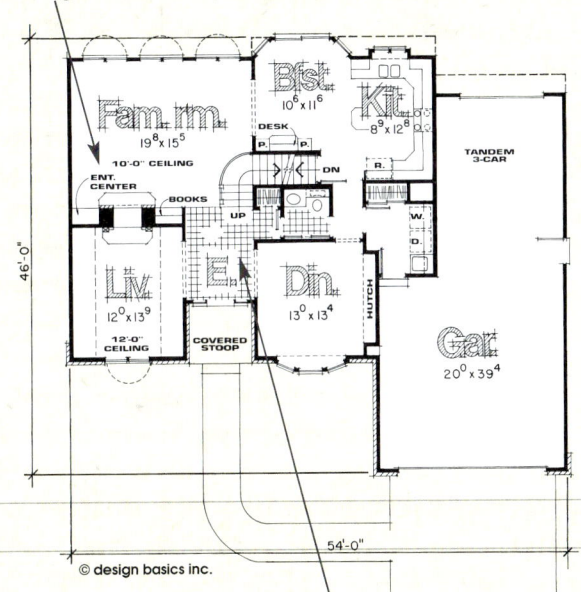

Spacious entry provides view of arched, transom-topped windows in the family room.

Master suite features tiered ceiling, 2-person whirlpool and huge, walk-in closet.

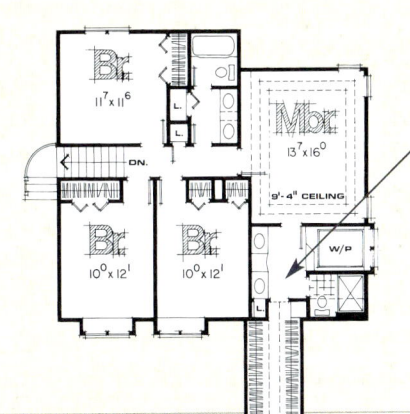

Main: 1204 SQ. FT.
Second: 1075 SQ. FT.
Total: 2279 SQ. FT.

ORDER DIRECT - (800) 947-7526   www.designbasics.com

This home may have been altered from the plan's original design.

BUILT BY: MJJ Construction

#44M-1868 *Price Code 18*

Somerset

#44M-2638 *Price Code 21*

Linden

BUILT BY: Rockland Homes

This home may have been altered from the plan's original design.

Three windows and a fireplace define the great room, along with a half wall allowing a view into the kitchen and breakfast area.

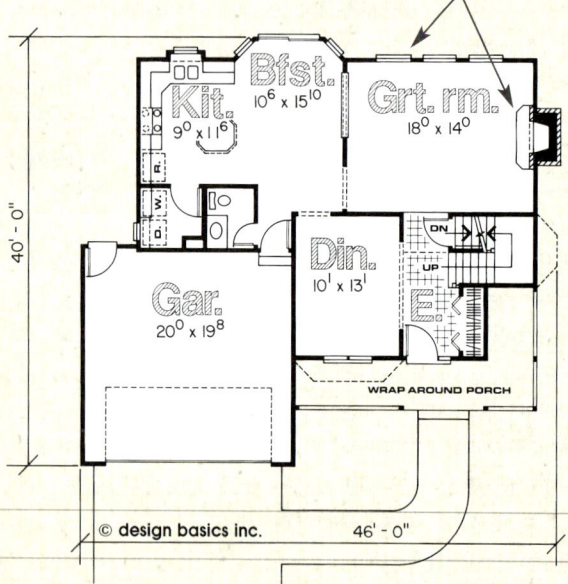

The parlor is located just inside the entry and makes a great, private area to relax.

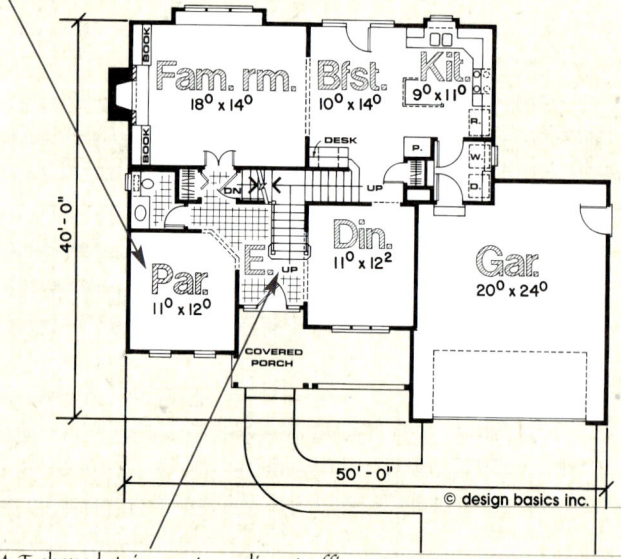

Bayed windows draw one up the stairway and to a second-floor balcony overlooking the entry.

His and her walk-in closets, a tiered ceiling and full bath with whirlpool tub are features that pamper in the master suite.

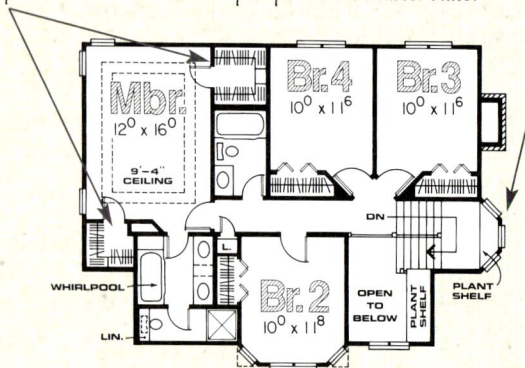

A T-shaped staircase streamlines traffic flow to the second floor.

An indented doorway into the walk-in closet of the master suite is the perfect place for a three-way mirror.

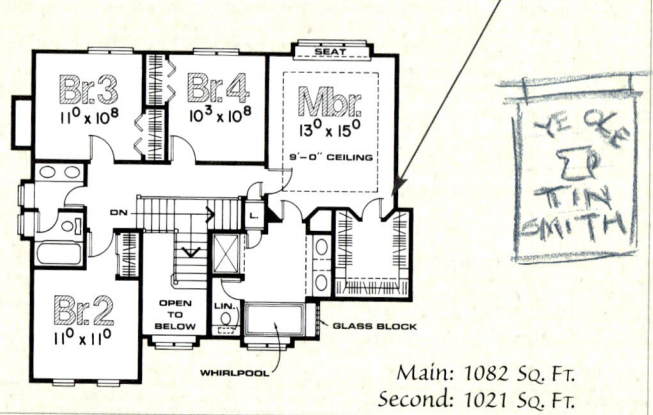

Main: 919 sq. ft.
Second: 923 sq. ft.
Total: 1842 sq. ft.

Main: 1082 sq. ft.
Second: 1021 sq. ft.
Total: 2103 sq. ft.

IMPRESSIONS — *Homes & Places for Real People*

BUILT BY: Ed Bedel Construction, Inc.

This home may have been altered from the plan's original design.

Gainsborough

#44M-2043   *Price Code* 32

The family room is anything but traditional with built-in entertainment center, bookshelves and stunning windows that stretch to the ceiling.

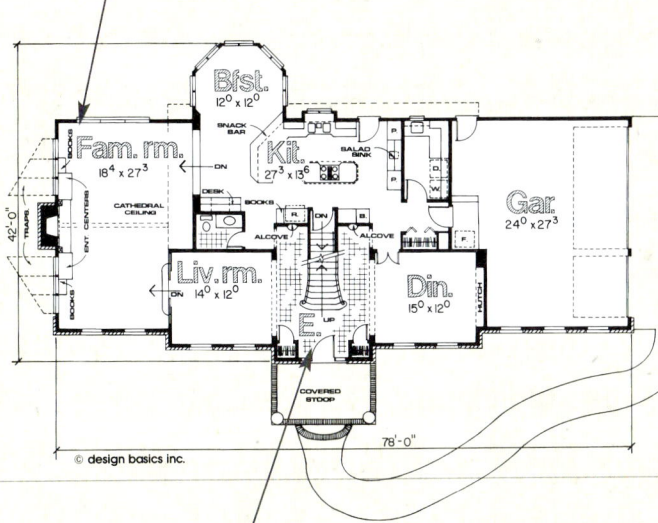

A traditional entry, with central stairway and formal rooms to each side, suits the Southern Colonial styling of its exterior.

The sloped ceiling and window seat in bedroom 4 make a quaint area a child will enjoy.

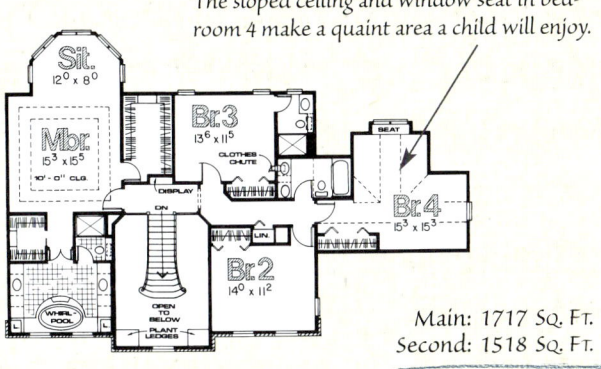

Main: 1717 Sq. Ft.
Second: 1518 Sq. Ft.

Total: 3235 Sq. Ft.

Ashton

#44M-2203   *Price Code* 23

BUILT BY: RLR Construction

This home may have been altered from the plan's original design.

A walk-in pantry and island counter equip this kitchen, open to a comfortable, sunny breakfast area.

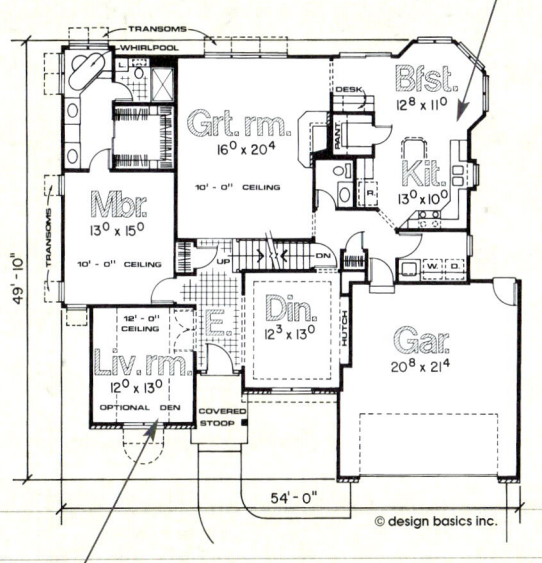

The living room easily converts to a den with double doors from the entry.

Main: 1697 Sq. Ft.
Second: 694 Sq. Ft.

Total: 2391 Sq. Ft.

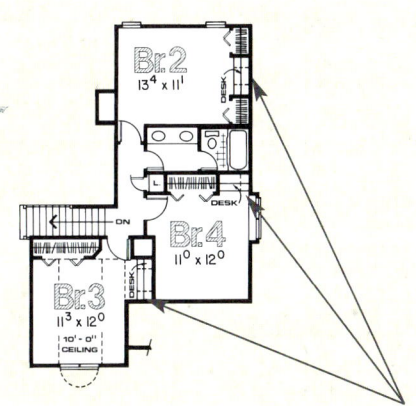

Built-in desks are a practical addition to all three secondary bedrooms.

ORDER DIRECT - (800) 947-7526   www.designbasics.com

Design Quality #2

A. The Bristol
B. The Kelsey
C. The Sedona

Timeless Charm...

Some things are always in style: Pearl necklaces, cardigan sweaters and long stemmed roses... Well-shined shoes, a firm handshake and polished manners... Baseball caps, the Three Stooges and classic Mustangs... A cheeseburger, fries and Coke for lunch... Sending Valentines, shooting fireworks on the 4th and writing letters to Santa Claus. In the same way, the time-honored details in these homes give them a sense of tradition and an appeal that's ageless.

3 Views...

A. Gingerbread details on the Bristol's exterior will make you feel like you're stepping back in time. The sense of nostalgia continues inside in the parlor with its large bayed window and sloped ceiling and the adjoining dining room. Captivating touches upstairs include skylights in both bathrooms and a porthole window above the staircase.

B. A quaint, gabled porch with an arch that traces a special window gives the Kelsey an alluring focal point. Inside, special details include bowed windows in the breakfast area, an angled hallway off the bedrooms, a boxed ceiling in the master bedroom, glass shelves over the tub and an eleven-foot-high ceiling in the great room.

C. A trio of gables, arched windows with quaint shutters and a graceful porch combine to give the Sedona its appealing exterior. The tall, sloped ceiling in the great room draws attention to the lovely fireplace flanked by transom-topped windows.

BUILT BY: Fornwald Construction

A. Bristol

Main: 1113 Sq. Ft.
Second: 965 Sq. Ft.
Total: 2078 Sq. Ft.

#44M-1870   Price Code 20

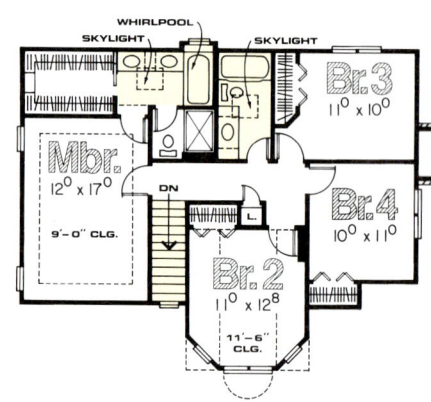

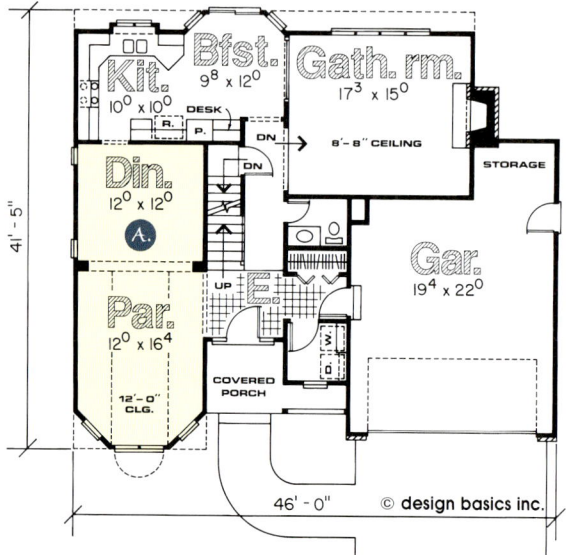

Dear Santa, All I want for Christmas is a football. David

IMPRESSIONS - *Homes & Places for Real People*

B. Kelsey

#44M-3019 Price Code 14

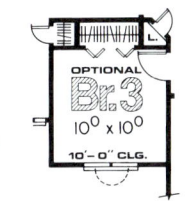

1479 Finished Sq. Ft.

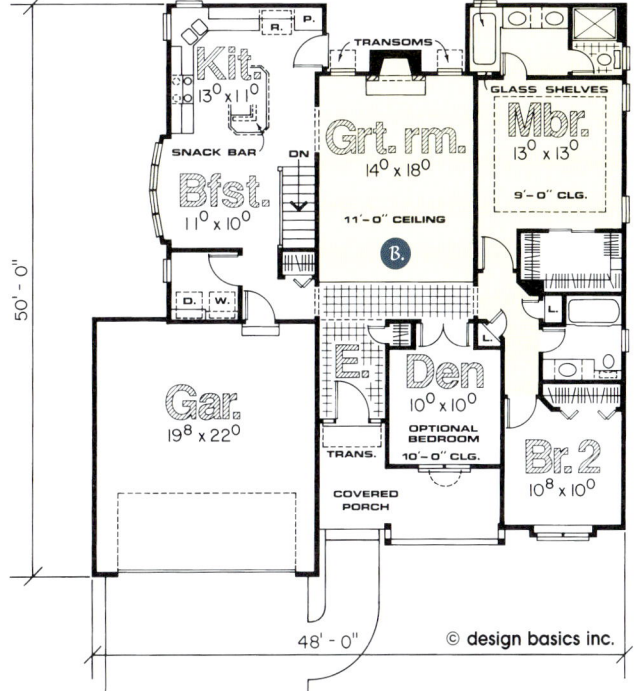

BUILT BY: Decker Building Company

ORDER DIRECT - (800) 947-7526   www.designbasics.com

BUILT BY: Artistic Homes

C. Sedona

#44M-5151 *Price Code* 17

Main: 1331 SQ. FT.
Second: 424 SQ. FT.

Total: 1755 SQ. FT.

NOTE: 9 ft. main level walls

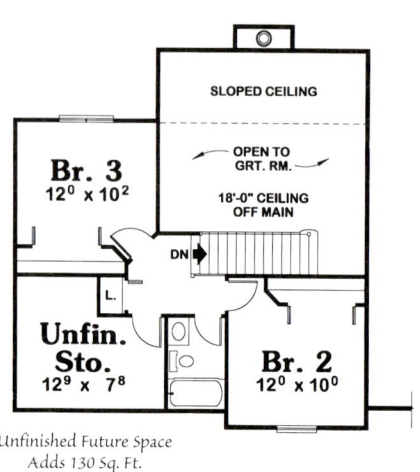

Unfinished Future Space
Adds 130 Sq. Ft.

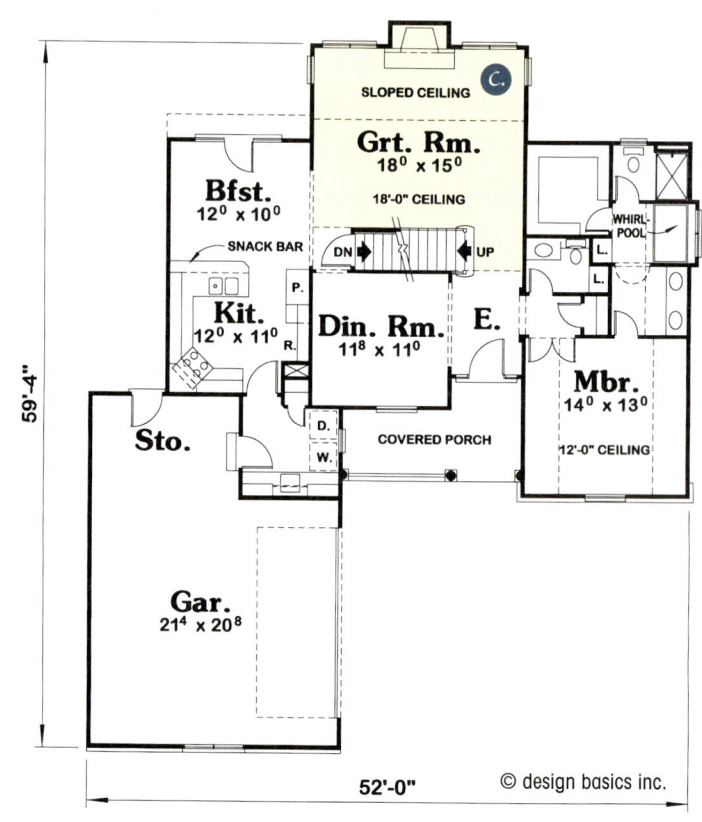

IMPRESSIONS - *Homes & Places for Real People*

This home may have been altered from the plan's original design.

BUILT BY: Timberlake Development

Monterey

#44M-2290 Price Code 16

#44M-2212 Price Code 17

Seville

This home may have been altered from the plan's original design.

BUILT BY: Mark Hughes Construction

A rear covered porch makes a great getaway off the breakfast area.

The dining room can expand into the great room when serving large groups.

The openness between the dining and great rooms is beneficial when hosting large groups.

A relaxing whirlpool tub and bayed window in the master suite could become favorite places to unwind.

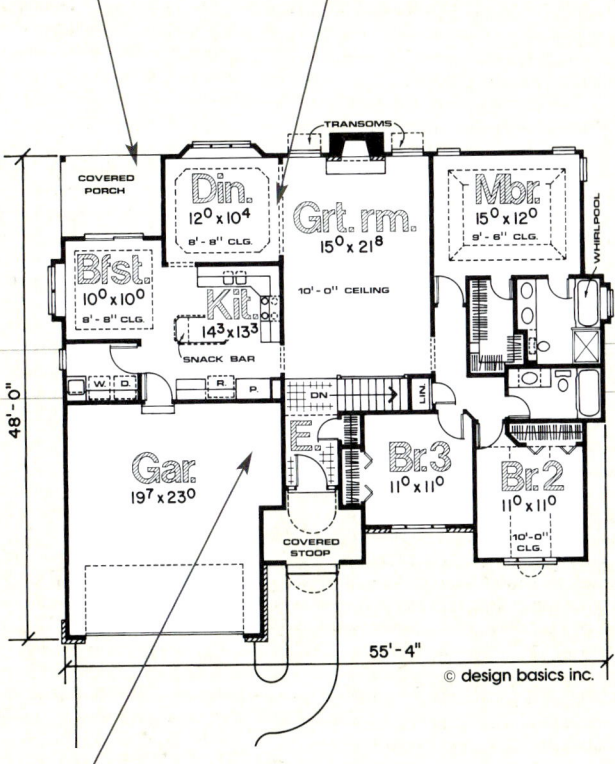

An alcove in the garage would be an ideal spot for storage shelves.

1666 Finished Sq. Ft.

An island counter helps organize the kitchen.

1735 Finished Sq. Ft.

ORDER DIRECT — (800) 947-7526   www.designbasics.com

The Midwest

A patchwork quilt, each square more striking than the last: Infinite horizons of subtle beauty. A sea of grass waving in the wind. Rich, black fields with rows of amber wheat and green corn stalks. Six-foot-high sunflowers. Overalls drying on a clothesline. A herd of cows roaming the pasture. Farmers harvesting their crops. Roadside stands with homegrown tomatoes, cucumbers, and sweet corn. A whirlwind of Canadian geese headed south. A cheery, chubby snow man and his entire family.

Where gray-haired couples dance the polka, church potlucks are giant smorgasbords, children address elders as "Ma'am" or "Sir" and help with chores after supper, volunteers deliver Meals on Wheels to shut-ins, neighbors gather at block parties and Old Glory waves on front porches.

A land of pioneers— from courageous homesteaders to today's Midwesterners conquering new challenges with hard work, inventiveness and perseverance. They're rich in tradition, too, with ethnic foods like dumplings and sauerkraut, ludefisk and lefse... herbal home remedies handed down from one generation to the next... hayrack rides and antique car parades... county fairs, fiddle festivals and Native American Powwows.

Heartland folks are down-to-earth people with bedrock values who know how to have fun: Fishing for walleyes. Hunting ring-necked pheasants. Playing hockey and soccer. Riding horses, mountain bikes or Harleys. Racing snowmobiles and hot air balloons. Going to Branson to see their favorite country entertainer. Sitting down to a home cooked meal and "shooting the breeze" with family and friends.

IMPRESSIONS— *Homes & Places for Real People*

BUILT BY: Mongold Construction Inc.

A. Patagonia

#44M-5086 *Price Code 24*

Main: 1162 Sq. Ft.
Second: 1255 Sq. Ft.

Total: 2417 Sq. Ft.

NOTE: 9 ft. main level walls

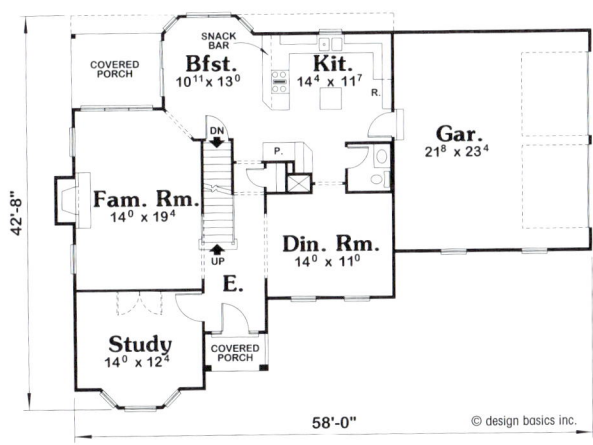

Unfinished Storage Adds 198 Sq. Ft.

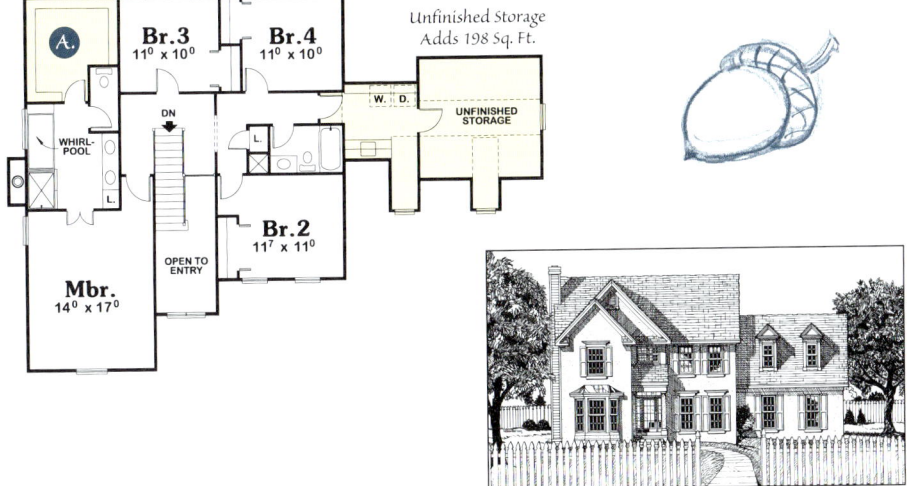

Design Quality #3

A. The Patagonia
B. The Adair
C. The Briarwood

Midwestern Practicality...

Few things are more precious than time. It can't be recycled; once it's used, it's gone. Unfortunately, we often use so much time on the things that seem urgent that we don't have enough left for the things that are really important: Spending time with family and friends. Spiritual renewal. Exercise and relaxation. Wouldn't it be great to have a home which helped you use your time better–with a convenient traffic flow to save steps, plenty of room for organized storage and flexible rooms to use to your best advantage?

3 Views...

A. Lack of storage space will never be an excuse in the Patagonia, with a large walk-in closet off the master bedroom and an unfinished storage room over the garage. Washing clothes will be easier, too, with a laundry room located on the upper level near all the bedrooms.

B. Efficiency comes naturally with the Adair. Bringing in groceries from the garage is just a short trip to the kitchen. The dining room is right next door to the kitchen and a wet bar is conveniently located between the dining room and breakfast area.

C. The Briarwood has a sunny office off the breakfast area which could also be used for exercise or hobbies. The spacious laundry room offers a built-in folding table. And a mud room and half bath just inside from the garage allow for quick clean-ups before coming into the rest of the home.

ORDER DIRECT – (800) 947-7526 www.designbasics.com

BUILT BY: Tweedt Engineering & Construction

B. Adair

#44M-2300   Price Code 14

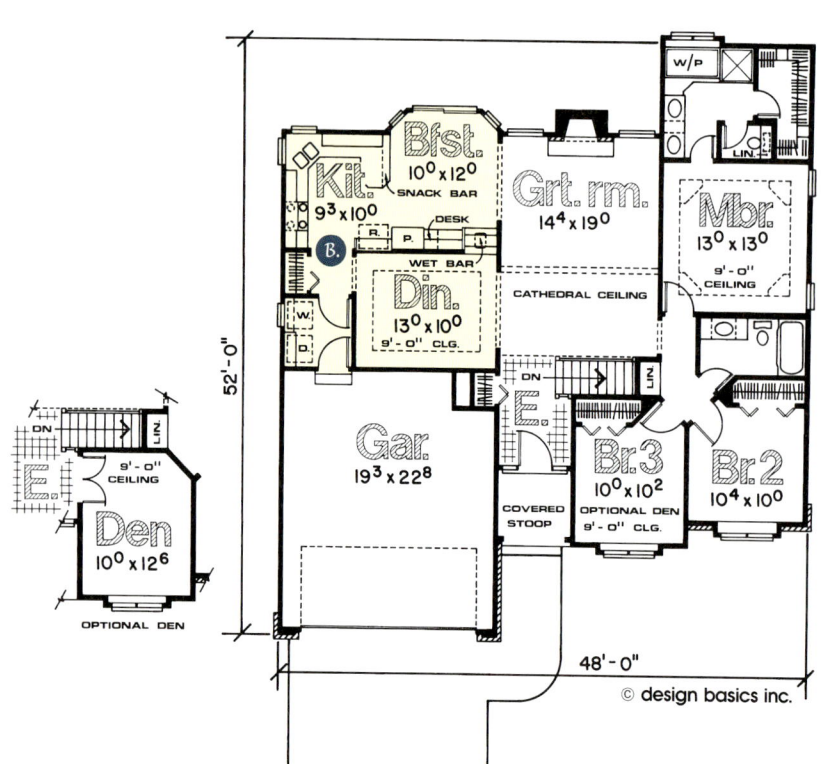

1496 Finished Sq. Ft.

IMPRESSIONS— *Homes & Places for Real People*

BUILT BY: Lucente & Sons Construction

C. Briarwood

#44M-2956   *Price Code 25*

Main: 1875 Sq. Ft.
Second: 687 Sq. Ft.

Total: 2562 Sq. Ft.

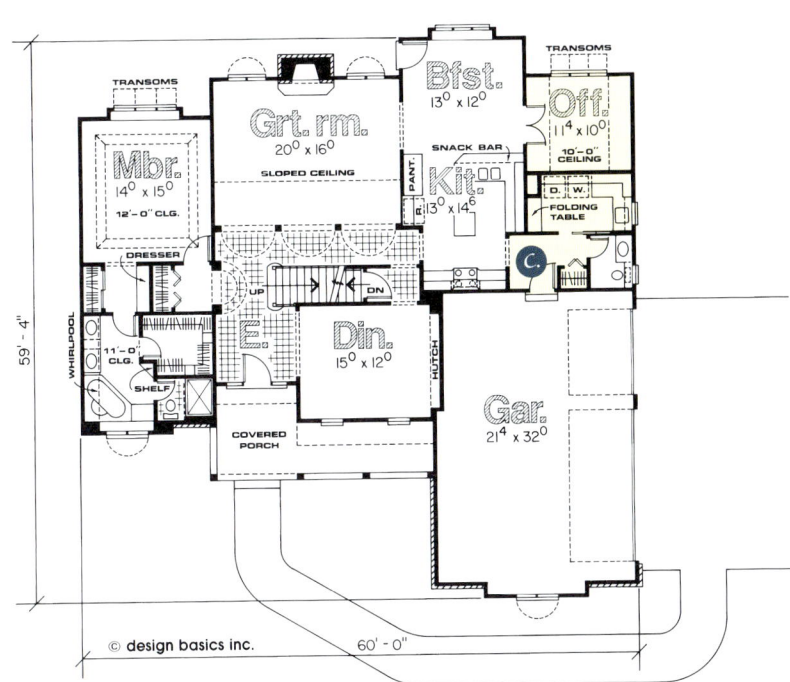

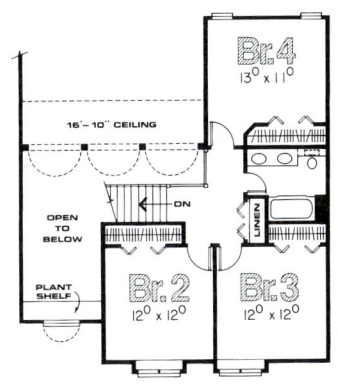

ORDER DIRECT - (800) 947-7526   www.designbasics.com

Home Owner Impressions

on Living in the Lawrence

BUILT BY: Kendel Hom

Pam and Mark were both farm kids who grew up in the same small town in Nebraska. After they married, Pam went on to become a special ed teacher; Mark became a district sales manager for an agricultural chemical company.

Except for five years in North Dakota, they've remained in their home state. A few years ago Mark began talking about building a home in the country. Pam dragged her feet. They'd lived in the home they were in for ten years. The house was rich with memories; their two teenage sons spent most of their childhood there. Furthermore, Pam didn't want to leave their wonderful neighbors.

As she considered the idea, Pam realized there were valid reasons to move. When he wasn't on the road, Mark worked at home from an office in an upstairs bedroom. The whole household was disrupted by phone calls, the fax machine and visitors walking through the house. The home's basement was unfinished, and although they considered remodeling, it wasn't large enough for a study and the family room they also wanted.

Once they made the decision to build, Mark and Pam began searching for a suitable location. They found it in a brand new development a few miles outside the city where each lot had two to four acres. Next, they started going to open houses to find the right home. It wasn't long before they chose the plan they would build– Design Basics' "Lawrence."

They've lived in their new home for two years. During that time many other homes have joined theirs in the development and Pam is

continued on page 26

Lawrence

#44M-2652 *Price Code 25*

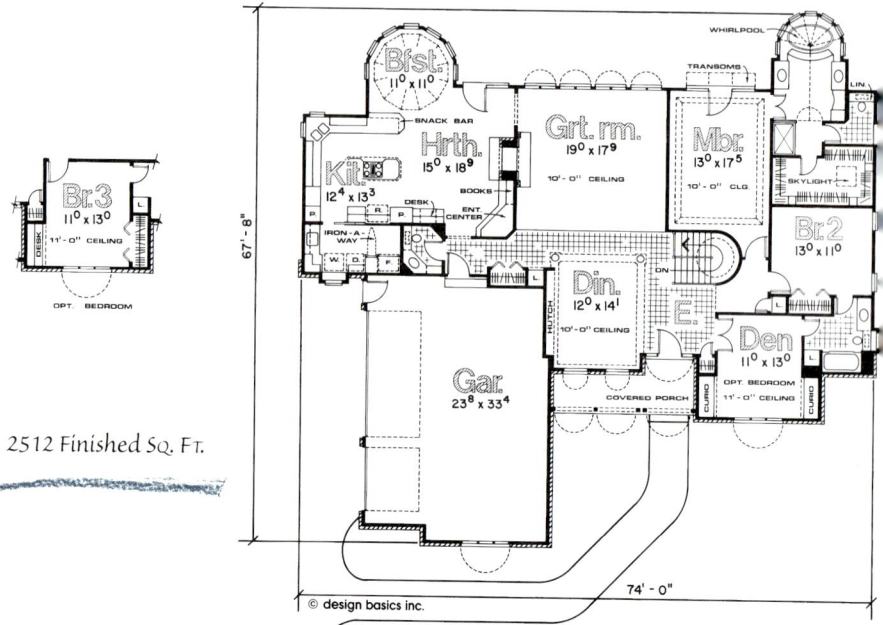

2512 Finished Sq. Ft.

BUILT BY: Roth Construction

Norris Crossing

#44M-8052 *Price Code 23*

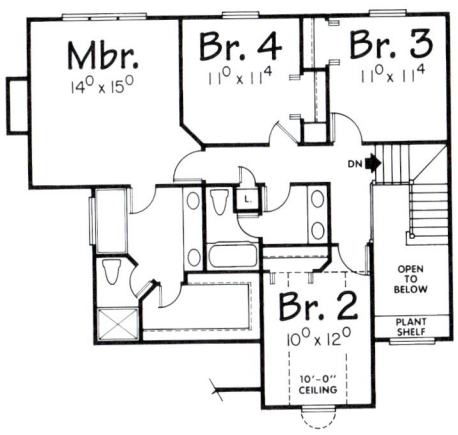

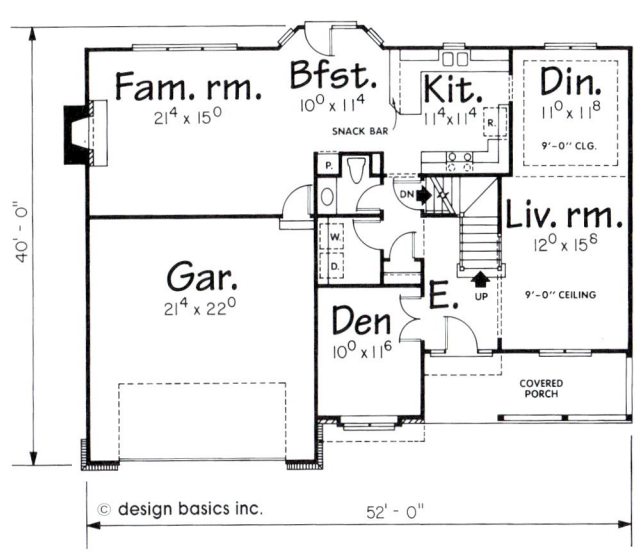

Main: 1269 Sq. Ft.
Second: 1034 Sq. Ft.

Total: 2303 Sq. Ft.

ORDER DIRECT - (800) 947-7526   www.designbasics.com

now convinced they did the right thing. "We enjoy life in the country," she says. "It's so peaceful and quiet. You notice the stars and the moon and the sunset a lot more. We have a screened porch which faces a creek with a lot of trees. In the morning we take our coffee and go out there and read the paper."

"We all love the outdoors," Pam continues. "Our family plays volleyball and croquet. We have a bonfire pit and plan to put in a horseshoe pit. The boys are always out playing basketball or, in our lot's wooded area, camping out."

The Lawrence also suits their family well. Mark uses the den as an office. When he meets with business associates at the house, they just come in the front door and the office is right there. With the office, master bedroom and laundry all on the main level, Pam expects this home to fit their needs indefinitely. She praises the practical floor plan. "Every space is so useable. Even though it's a larger home, it doesn't give you an empty feeling at all. It doesn't seem like we've wasted any space."

Friends compliment Pam's cozy country style of decorating and the home's kitchen area. With a large island snack bar that easily seats four, the breakfast nook, and the hearth room, it provides the perfect setting for small gatherings.

Mark and Pam's lot accommodated a walkout basement giving them a bright, roomy lower level. They divided this additional space into an entertainment area, a bedroom for each son, a guest room, a bathroom and a computer room. With one son a freshman in high school and other a freshman in college, they're at an age to appreciate having their own space to have friends over and shoot pool. The lower level also has a storm shelter. "Being out in the country in Nebraska, we thought that would be a good thing," Pam says. "And it has come in handy at times."

According to Pam, there's only drawback to living in their new home in the country: hearing Mark say, "I told you so."

Jefferson

#44M- 2890 Price Code 17

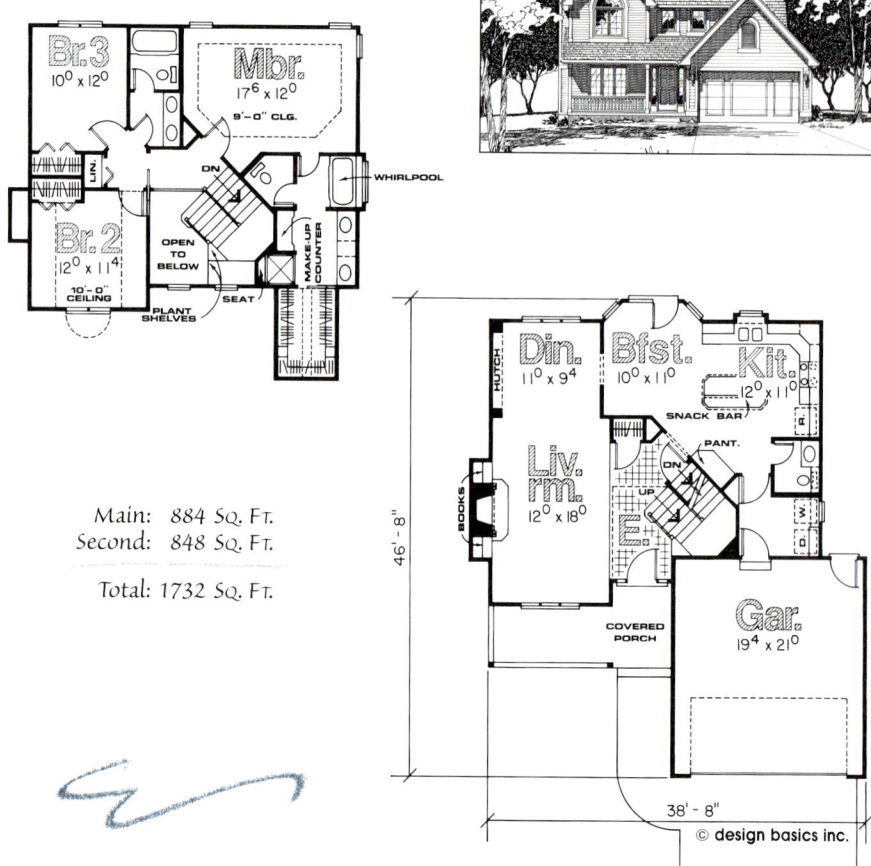

Main: 884 SQ. FT.
Second: 848 SQ. FT.

Total: 1732 SQ. FT.

IMPRESSIONS- *Homes & Places for Real People*

BUILT BY: Lexmark Homes

Fairview

#44M-24015   Price Code 27

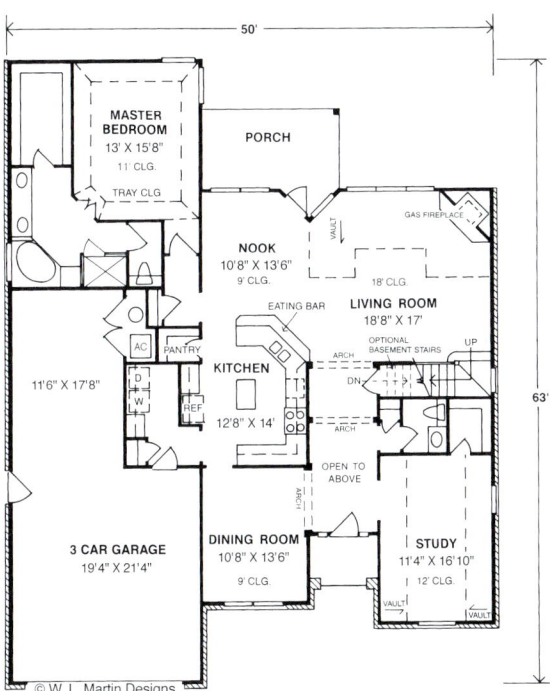

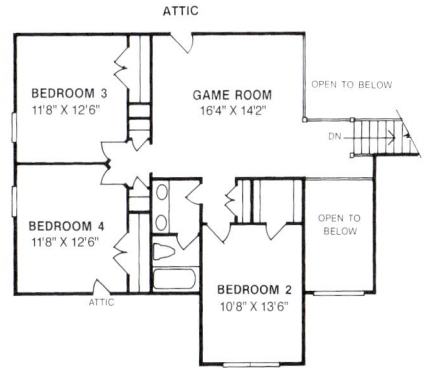

Main: 1830 SQ. FT.
Second: 925 SQ. FT.

Total: 2755 SQ. FT.

NOTE: 9 ft. main level walls

ORDER DIRECT - (800) 947-7526   www.designbasics.com

BUILT BY: Hollander Homes

This home may have been altered from the plan's original design.

Albany

#44M-2235 Price Code 19

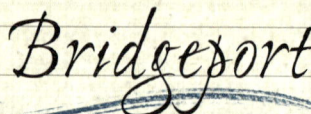
#44M-2460 Price Code 26

Bridgeport

BUILT BY: Golba Construction

This home may have been altered from the plan's original design.

One of the most enjoyable aspects of this great room will be the amount of light brought in by front and rear windows with transoms above.

Plenty of storage in the garage allows space for a work center and bike and equipment storage.

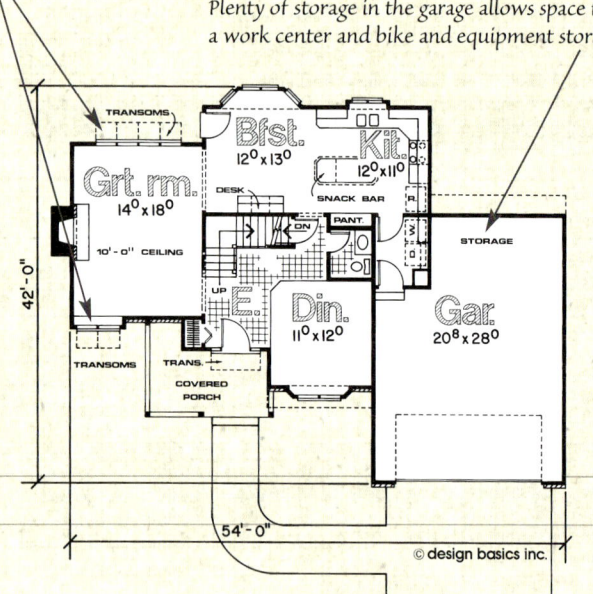

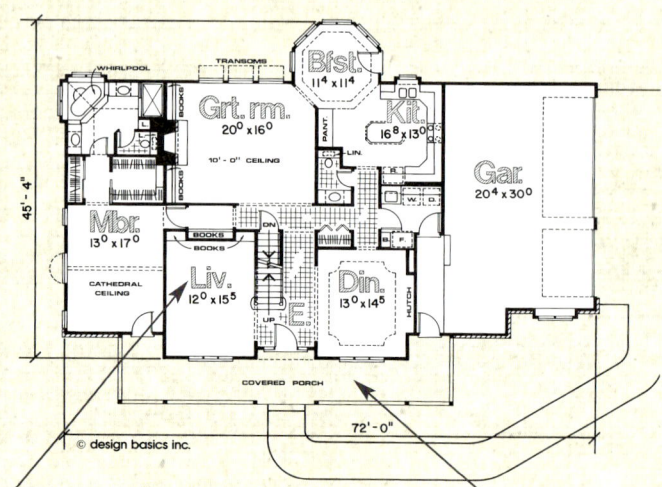

With its built-in bookshelves, the living room easily converts into a den or office.

Spanning the front of the home, a deep porch has access from the master suite and garage.

Main: 944 Sq. Ft.
Second: 987 Sq. Ft.

Total: 1931 Sq. Ft.

Main: 1881 Sq. Ft.
Second: 814 Sq. Ft.

Total: 2695 Sq. Ft.

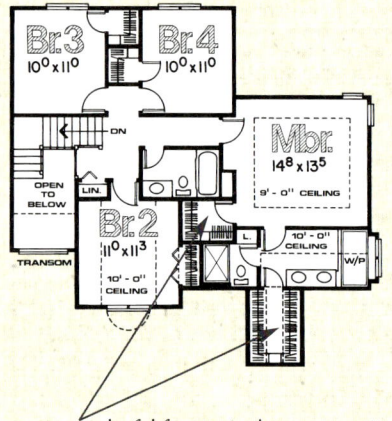

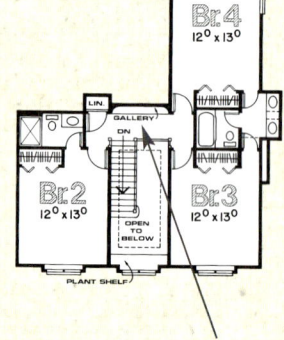

His and her walk-in closets are a wonderful feature in the master suite.

A display gallery on the second floor is highlighted in the two-story entry with boxed ceiling.

IMPRESSIONS— Homes & Places for Real People

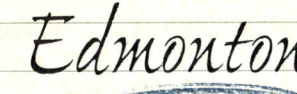
Edmonton

#44M-2309 *Price Code* 25

BUILT BY: Integrity Builders

This home may have been altered from the plan's original design.

BUILT BY: John Caniglia Builders

This home may have been altered from the plan's original design.

Ingram

#44M-2281 *Price Code* 17

The great room enhances any gathering with its high, sloped ceiling and fireplace flanked by windows.

A corner walk-in pantry and island counter benefit the hearth kitchen.

French doors and a built-in bookcase enhance the entrance to the master suite.

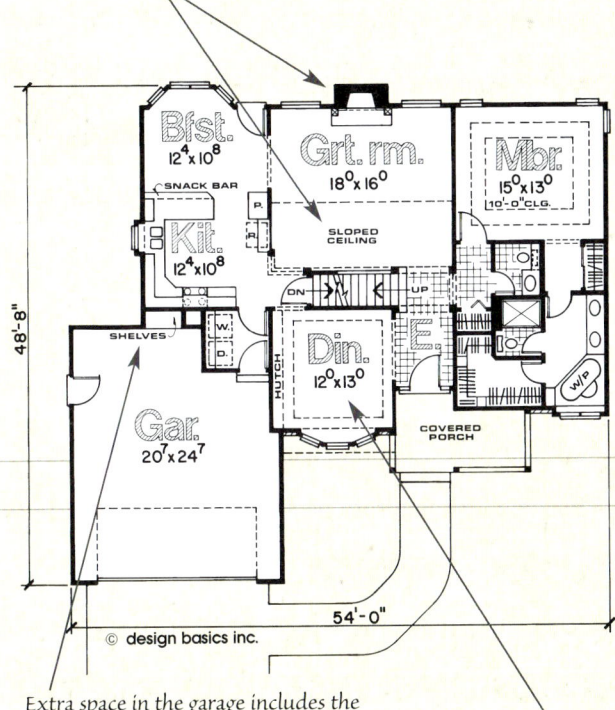

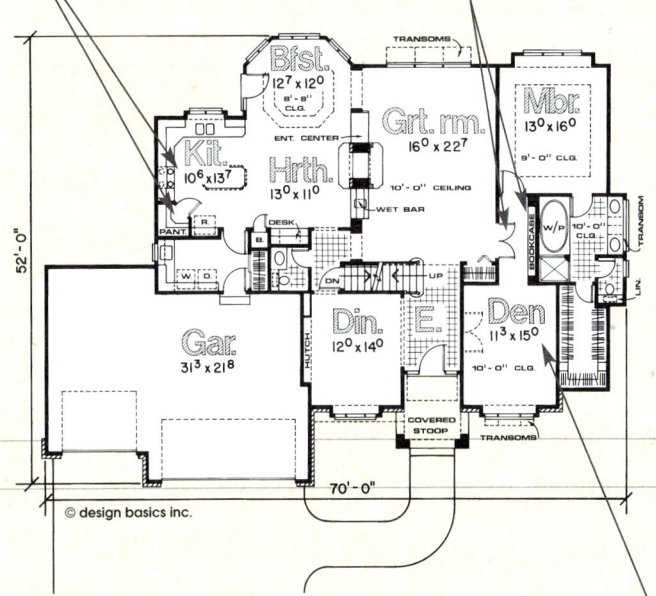

Extra space in the garage includes the convenience of built-in shelves.

A den with tall windows enjoys a private location near the master suite.

Meals are prepared just steps away from the formal bayed dining room.

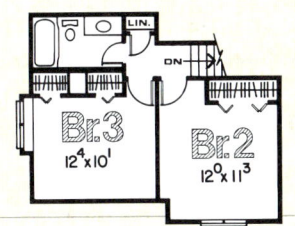

Main: 1348 SQ. FT.
Second: 430 SQ. FT.
Total: 1778 SQ. FT.

Main: 1933 SQ. FT.
Second: 646 SQ. FT.
Total: 2579 SQ. FT.

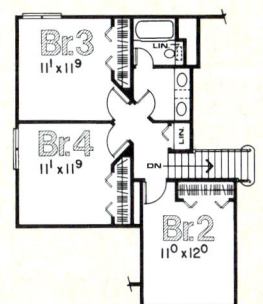

ORDER DIRECT — (800) 947-7526   www.designbasics.com   29

This home may have been altered from the plan's original design.

BUILT BY: Kendel Homes

Fayette

#44M-2346 *Price Code 24*

The sunken family room in this home is easily accessed from both the kitchen and entry.

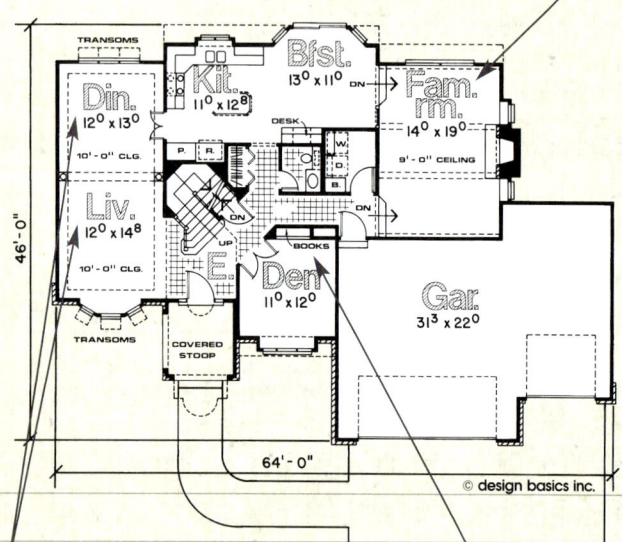

The living and dining rooms easily expand into each other when entertaining.

Built-in shelves offer a place to display mementos in the den.

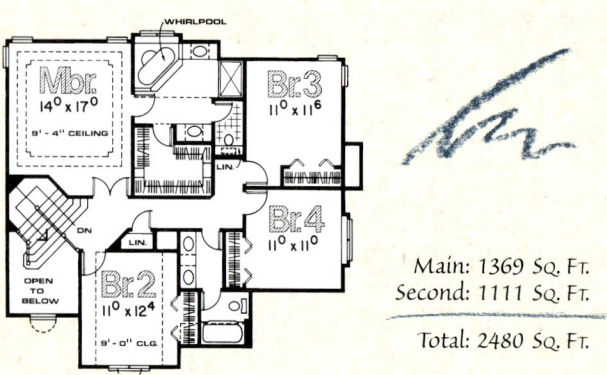

Main: 1369 SQ. FT.
Second: 1111 SQ. FT.
Total: 2480 SQ. FT.

Winrock

#44M-2746 *Price Code 27*

This home may have been altered from the plan's original design.

BUILT BY: Grubb Enterprises

Practical kitchen provides a pantry, 2 lazy Susans and large center work island.

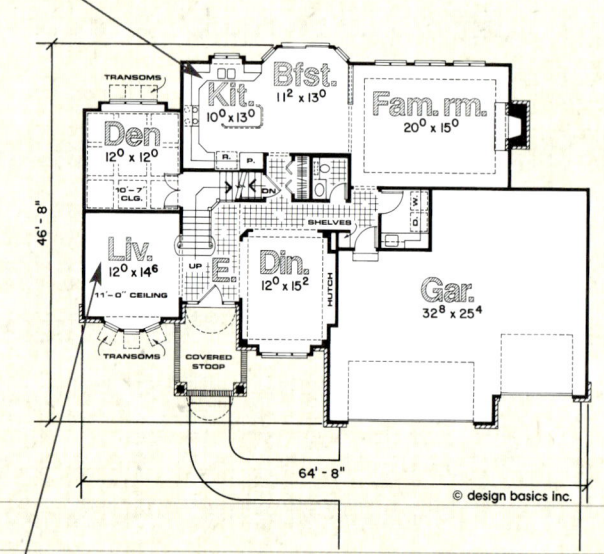

An eleven-foot-high ceiling and a large bayed window add elegance to the living room.

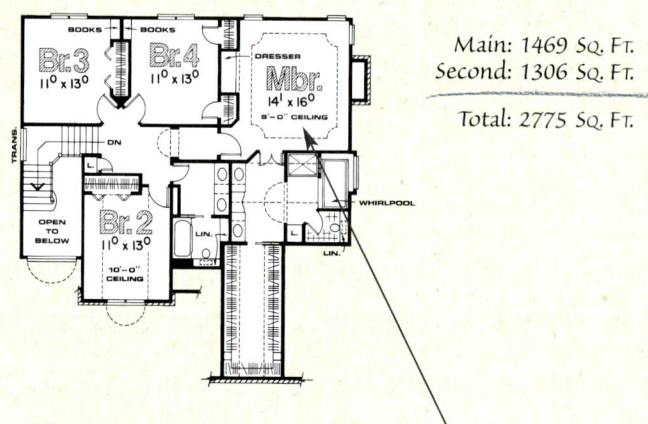

Main: 1469 SQ. FT.
Second: 1306 SQ. FT.
Total: 2775 SQ. FT.

Distinctive master suite is highlighted by built-in dresser, extra-large walk-in closet and luxurious bath with arched opening to whirlpool and shower area.

IMPRESSIONS— *Homes & Places for Real People*

BUILT BY: Wick Homes

This home may have been altered from the plan's original design.

Angel Cove

#44M-8094 *Price Code* 17

Bayed windows in the breakfast area provide a perfect view of the outdoors from the kitchen.

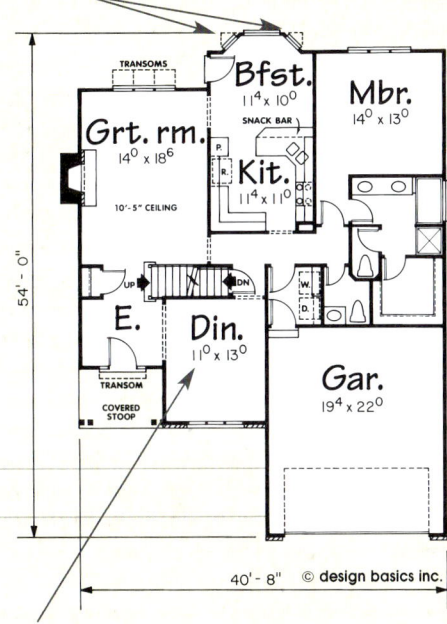

The dining room is within steps of the kitchen for convenience.

A future room on the second floor offers plenty of storage for seasonal and other items.

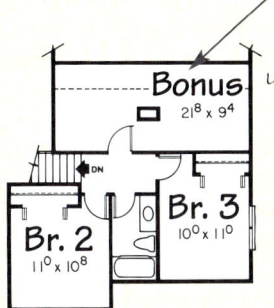

Main: 1324 SQ. FT.
Second: 391 SQ. FT.
Total: 1715 SQ. FT.

Curtiss

#44M-2401 *Price Code* 20

This home may have been altered from the plan's original design.

BUILT BY: Brody Construction

Bayed windows in the family room provide plenty of sunshine and a view to the backyard.

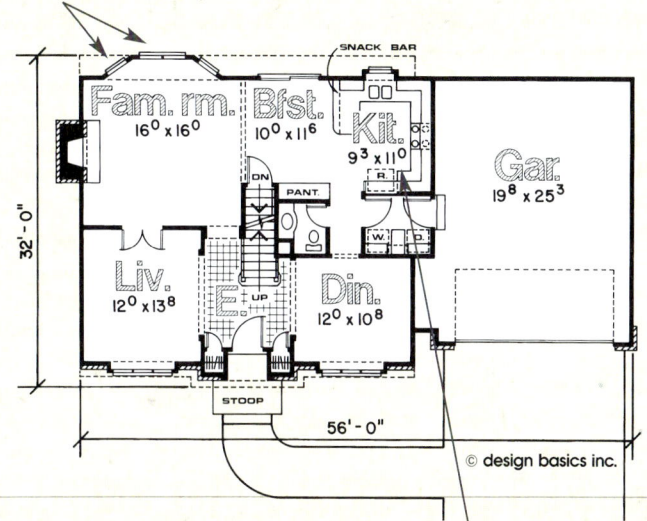

A proficient work area is established in the kitchen with a large window above the sink, a snack bar and roomy pantry.

A nine-foot, boxed ceiling and book shelf decorate the second-floor corridor that leads to the bedrooms.

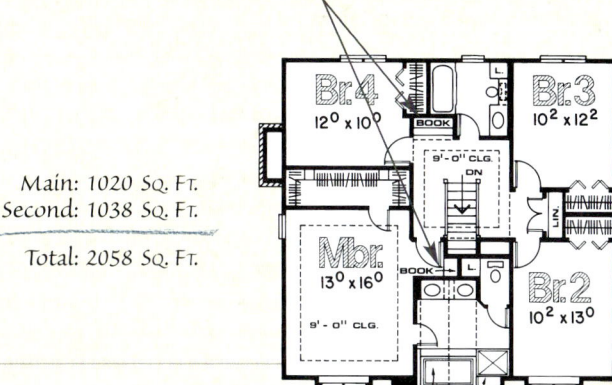

Main: 1020 SQ. FT.
Second: 1038 SQ. FT.
Total: 2058 SQ. FT.

Design Quality #4

- A. The Shawnee
- B. The Fairchild
- C. The Woodvine Manor

Wide Open Spaces...

Life is crowded—whether you live on a farm in Iowa or in a New York suburb. We write on each calendar square in tiny print so we can fit everything in. Our "to do" list is as thick as a big city phone book. We shuffle stacks of papers with things we have to remember. Our days are jammed with activities and our minds crowded with concerns. Imagine coming home to a house that helps you feel less squeezed. The open floor plans in these homes provide a feeling of spaciousness— beckoning your spirit to stretch out and unwind.

3 Views...

A. An unrestricted view from the entry into the dining and great rooms makes the Shawnee seem larger than it is. The great room, with a 10-foot-high ceiling, is open to the kitchen and breakfast area, contributing to the sense of roominess.

B. A dramatic staircase and balcony distinguish the Fairchild's grand entrance, while both the dining and living rooms are viewed from the front door. A large master bedroom opens to a generous sitting room. The family room, breakfast area and kitchen all flow together for unrestricted views.

C. Long views characterize the Woodvine Manor. From the family room you can see the whole length of the house through the living room, entry and dining room. A mid-level landing overlooks the family room, and an over-sized kitchen and breakfast area sustain the home's open feeling.

BUILT BY: RLR Construction

A. Shawnee

#44M-2461   Price Code 18

1850 Finished Sq. Ft.

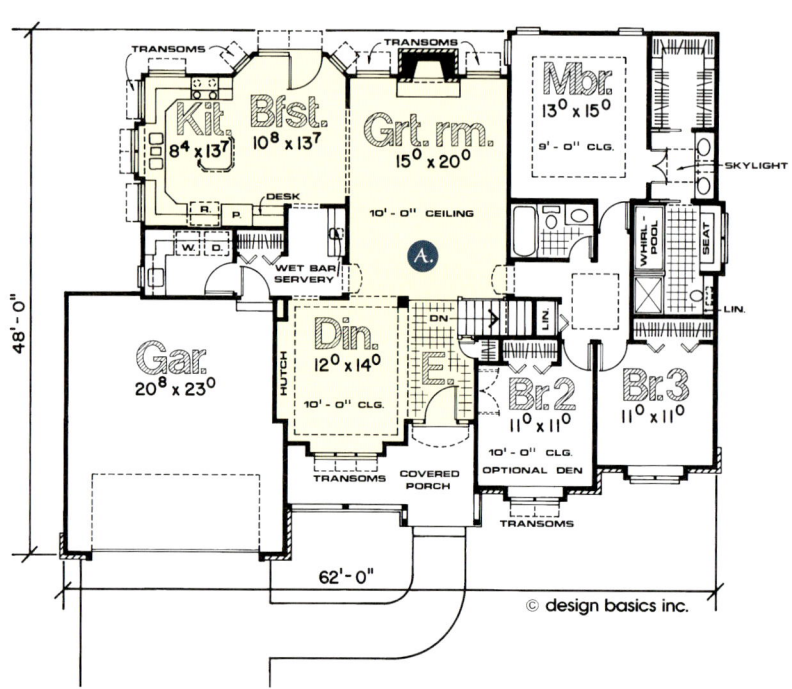

B. Fairchild

#44M-2733   Price Code 39

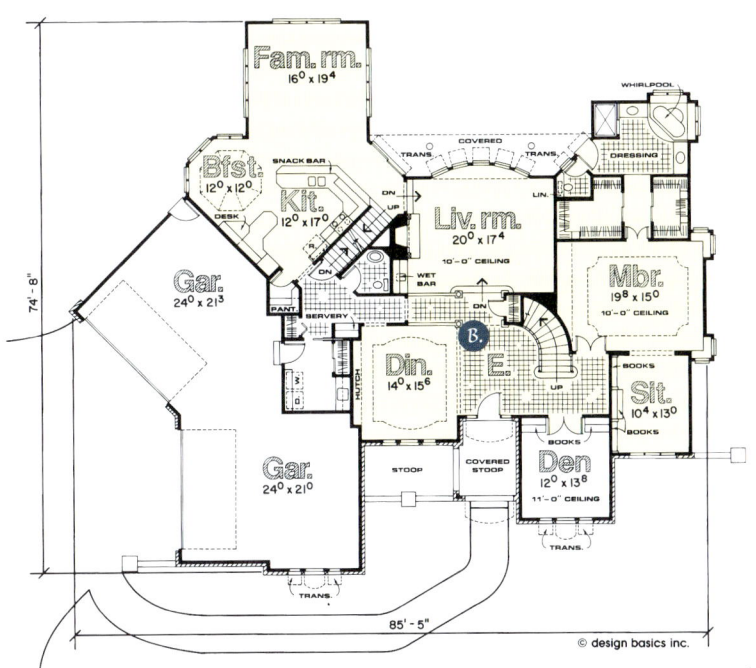

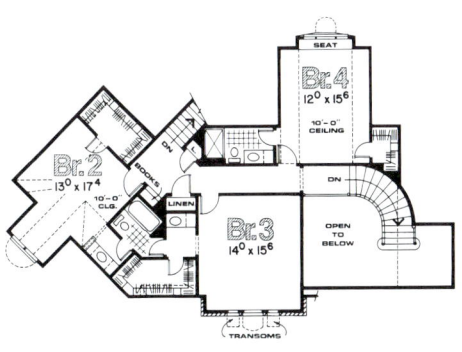

Main: 2813 Sq. Ft.
Second: 1091 Sq. Ft.

Total: 3904 Sq. Ft.

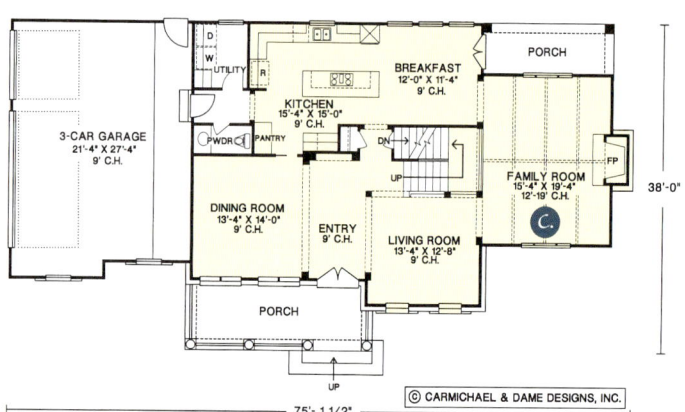

BUILT BY: O'Donnell Construction

C. Woodvine Manor

#44M-9161   *Price Code 27*

Main: 1400 SQ. FT.
Second: 1315 SQ. FT.

Total: 2715 SQ. FT.

NOTE: 9 ft. main level walls

IMPRESSIONS— *Homes & Places for Real People*

BUILT BY: Scott Fairmont Signature Homes

This home may have been altered from the plan's original design.

Thornhill

#44M-3494 *Price Code 28*

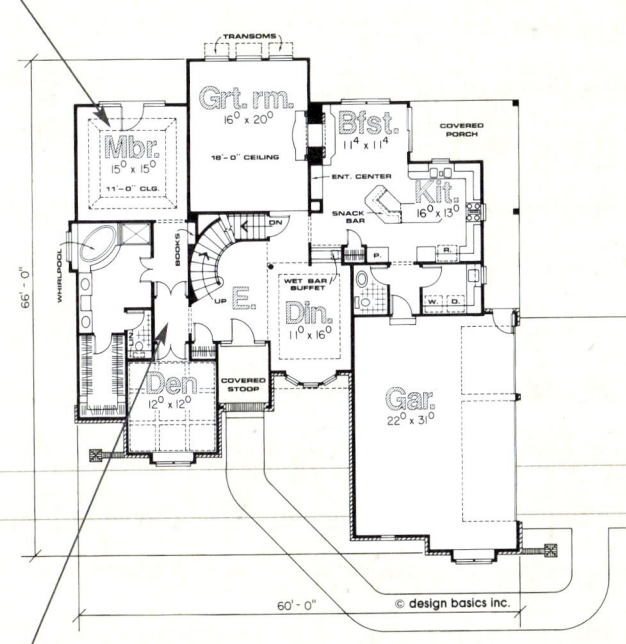

- A built-in bookcase, vaulted ceiling and door to the back enhance the relaxing master bedroom.
- A hallway just off the entry secludes the master suite and den in privacy.
- The dramatic great room can be viewed from a second-floor balcony.

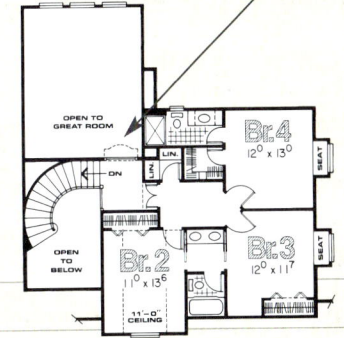

Main: 2041 SQ. FT.
Second: 809 SQ. FT.

Total: 2850 SQ. FT.

Crawford

#44M-2408 *Price Code 22*

This home may have been altered from the plan's original design.

BUILT BY: Oakmark Builders

- The openness between the kitchen, hearth room and breakfast area allows the family to interact while preparing dinner.
- A built-in entertainment center in the great room is convenient for home electronic equipment.

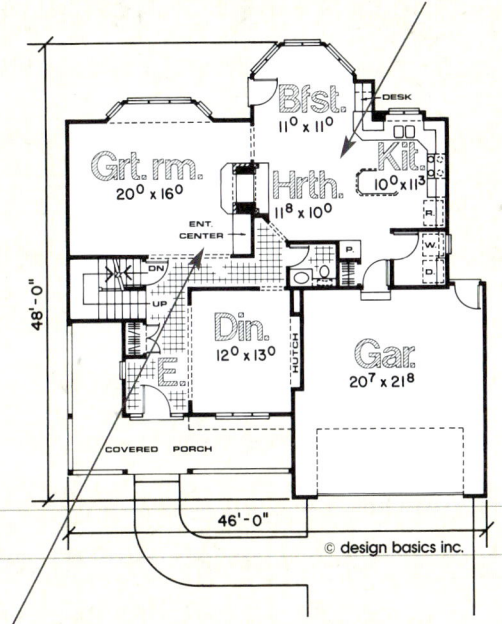

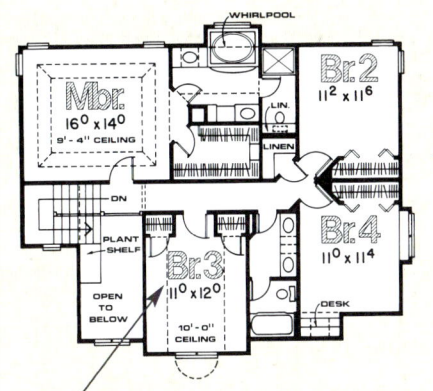

- Bedroom 3 has unique features, such as twin closets, an arched window and a 10-foot-high ceiling.

Main: 1150 SQ. FT.
Second: 1120 SQ. FT.

Total: 2270 SQ. FT.

ORDER DIRECT — (800) 947-7526 www.designbasics.com 35

The South

The kind of images peaceful dreams are made of: A secluded path through a dense pine forest. Rushing waterfalls. Misty cypress swamps. Sugar sand beaches. Majestic Appalachian mountains. Fields of cotton. Gardenias, azaleas, camellias, and wisteria. A horse-drawn carriage on a cobblestone street. Wrought iron and white picket fences. Lush, manicured gardens. Ornate fountains. Antebellum homes with stately columns. A paddlewheeler gliding down the river.

A land filled with the scent of peaches and honeysuckle and the sound of music. Where the Grand Ole Opry was born and music legends like Hank Williams, Elvis Presley, Ray Charles and the Allman Brothers touched the soul of a nation. Offering a rich diversity from the Atlanta opera and ballet to Dixieland jazz, mountain folk music, bluegrass, country, gospel, soul, rock and rhythm and blues.

A polite and friendly place. Where tea is served on lace tablecloths and one still dresses up to go to church... Ladies are genteel and soft spoken... Repairmen go out of their way to be helpful...People wait for an answer when they ask, "How are you?" ... And new neighbors are welcomed with warm gingerbread.

Most Southerners have learned life is too short to hurry through. They understand the importance of taking time to relax. Shooting nine holes of golf or playing a tennis match. White water rafting or hang gliding. Watching steeple chase or NASCAR races. Listening to a street musician. Fishing for largemouth bass. Lying on a sun drenched beach. Picnicking under a fragrant magnolia tree. Retreating to a hammock with a good book. Sipping a mint julep on the porch and savoring the good life.

BUILT BY: Jollar Inc.

Design Quality #5

A. The Jacksonville
B. The Tealwood Estate
C. The Greensboro

A. Jacksonville

#44M-3156 Price Code 32

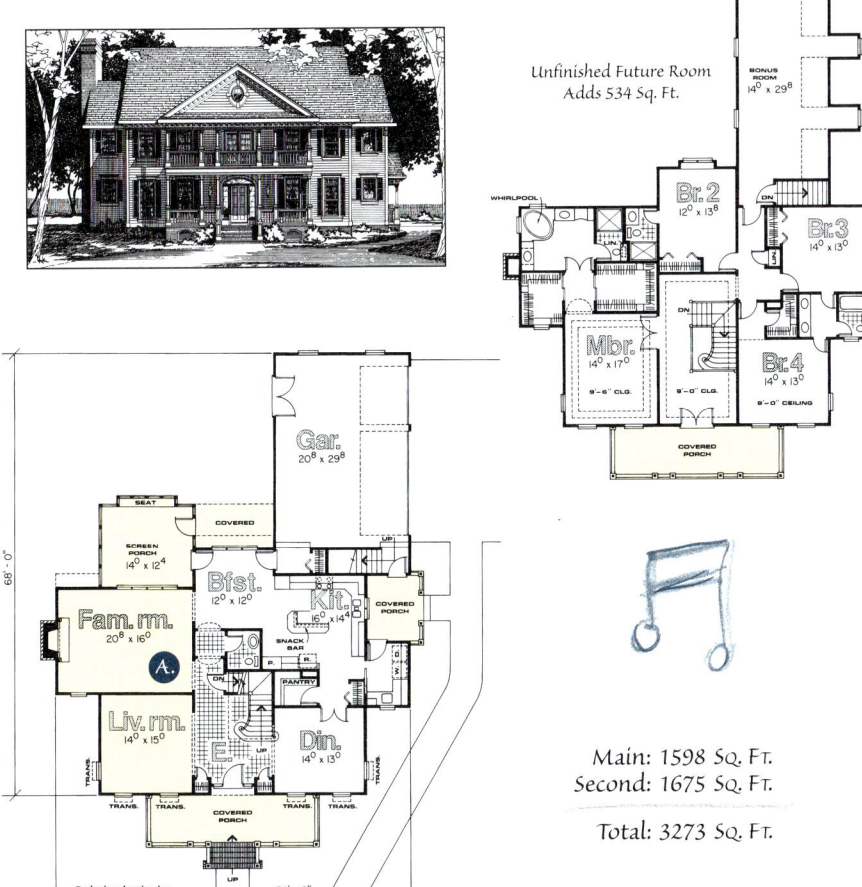

Main: 1598 Sq. Ft.
Second: 1675 Sq. Ft.

Total: 3273 Sq. Ft.

Southern Hospitality...

Gatherings of friends and family fill a home with warm memories. Children's birthday parties. Thanksgiving dinners with all the trimmings. Extended family opening gifts around the Christmas tree. Celebrations for a new job promotion or a soccer team winning the state championship. Super Bowl get-togethers. Coffee klatches. Graduation open houses. Bridal showers. Backyard barbecues and neighborhood potlucks. These homes are specially designed to help you entertain with ease and allow guests to mingle freely.

3 Views...

A. With countless places for guests to spread out, the Jacksonville easily accommodates big gatherings. In addition to a spacious family room and formal living and dining rooms, there are stacked porches on the front of the home, a screened porch with an adjoining covered porch in the back, plus a covered porch on the side.

B. A wide front porch welcomes visitors to the Tealwood Estate. A lovely fireplace and lofty cathedral ceiling make the family room warm and inviting. An open breakfast area and snack bar allow guests to circulate. And the roomy kitchen permits guests to pitch in or help themselves.

C. Company is sure to feel at home in the Greensboro– with a roomy dining and living room right across from each other and an impressive great room just a few steps away. Formal meals are simplified with a servery just outside the dining room and an ample pantry and island counter in the kitchen.

ORDER DIRECT - (800) 947-7526   www.designbasics.com

37

B. Tealwood Estate

#44M-9162 *Price Code 30*

Main: 2116 Sq. Ft.
Second: 956 Sq. Ft.

Total: 3072 Sq. Ft.

NOTE: 9 ft. main level walls

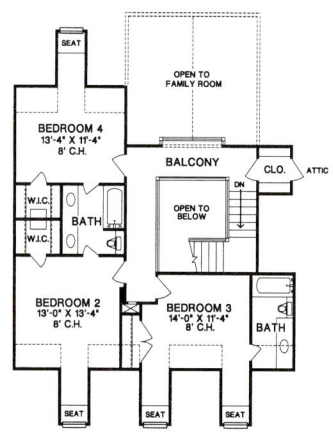

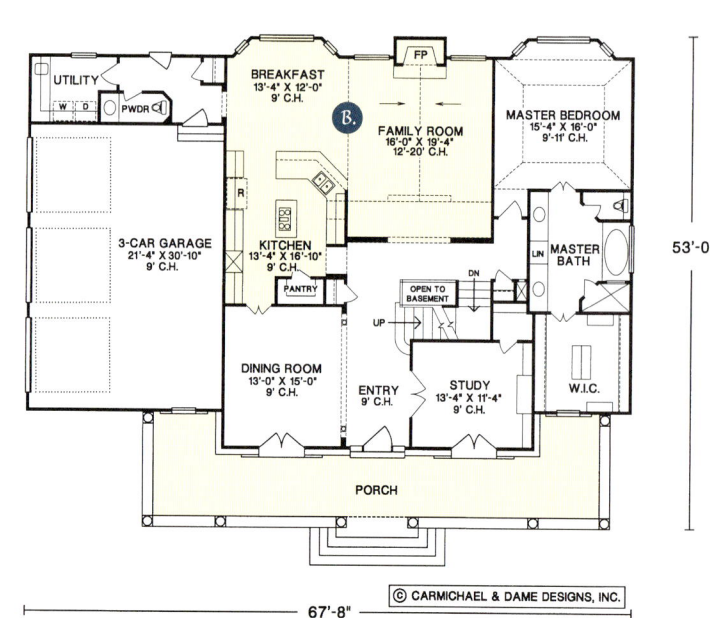

BUILT BY: Jarco Development

IMPRESSIONS— *Homes & Places for Real People*

BUILT BY: Lucente & Sons Construction

C. Greensboro

#44M-2326   Price Code 21

2172 Finished SQ. FT.

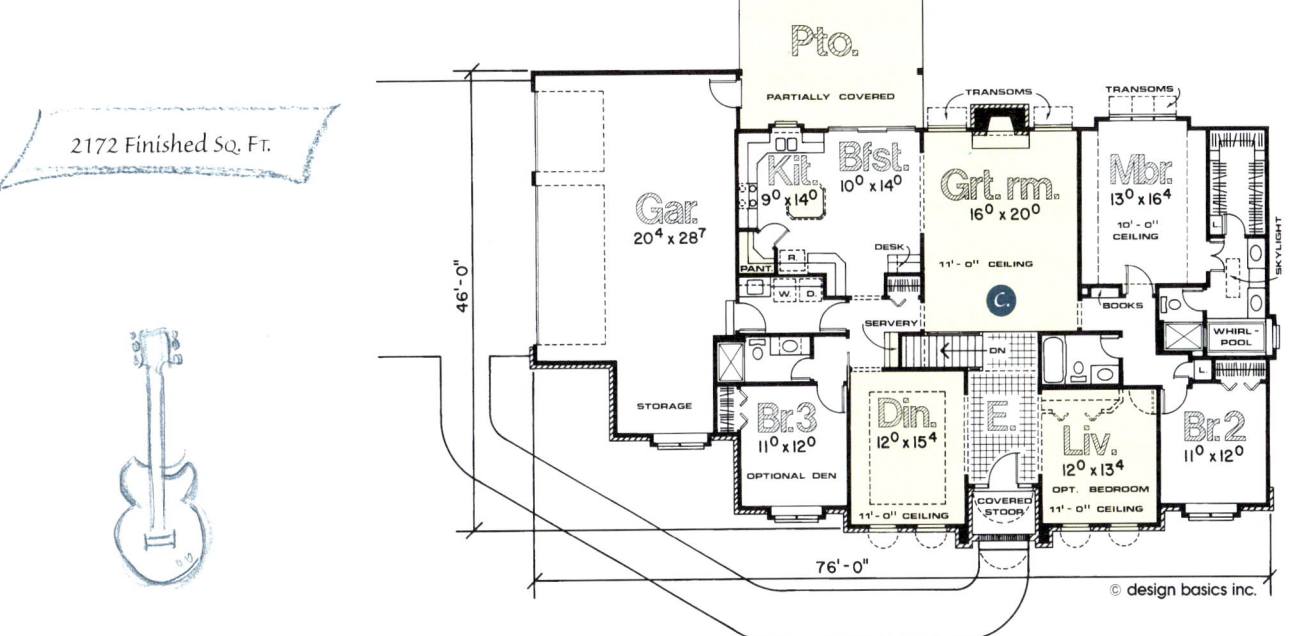

ORDER DIRECT - (800) 947-7526   www.designbasics.com   39

Home Owner Impressions

on living in the Winchester

BUILT BY: Landmark Homes

Bob and Edith lived in Alaska, Texas and Florida before moving to Alabama twenty years ago. They have come to love its ideal climate and beautiful scenery. With a son and daughter living in Tennessee, they travel back and forth to Nashville every other week. The drive is a visual feast with its abundance of trees, mountains and wild flowers.

Living in a college town gives them a wide variety of activities to enjoy. A grandson plays basketball for the University of North Alabama, so they rarely miss a game. They're also big Alabama football fans and enjoy the local theater.

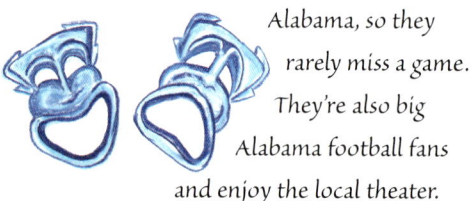

After twenty years in the paper industry, Bob and Edith are now semi-retired. Since they spend less time working, it was especially important that their home be a comfortable place. Three years ago they moved into Design Basics' "Winchester." The home is located in an exclusive neighborhood that boasts views of lush landscaping typical of the South: cypress and crape myrtle trees, azaleas, camellias, and lots of roses. Edith comments, "We love living in this area. We have a thick grove of pine trees behind us that is just beautiful. It's a very quiet community and the homes are all unique with gorgeous exteriors."

The views inside the home are equally stunning. Entering the front door, one immediately notices the dining room where a Persian rug

continued on page 42

Winchester

#44M-2475   Price Code 35

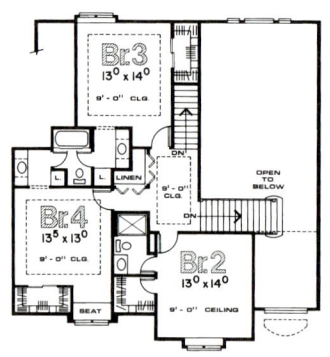

Main: 2555 Sq. Ft.
Second: 1001 Sq. Ft.

Total: 3556 Sq. Ft.

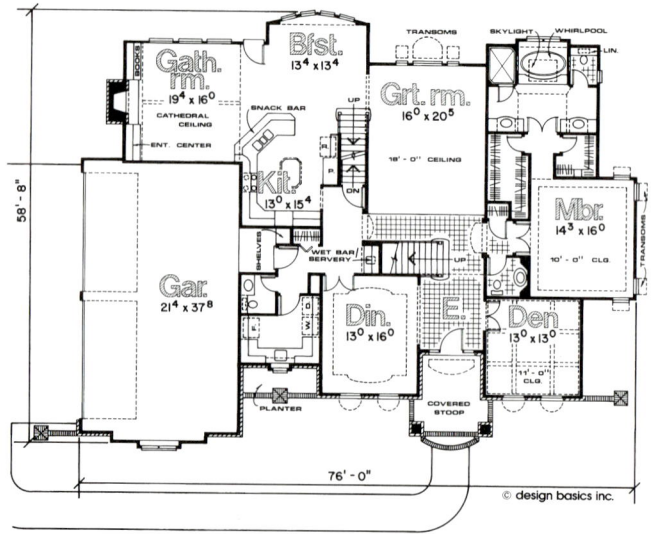

IMPRESSIONS — *Homes & Places for Real People*

BUILT BY: Wegher Construction

Pinehurst

#44M-2311 *Price Code 24*

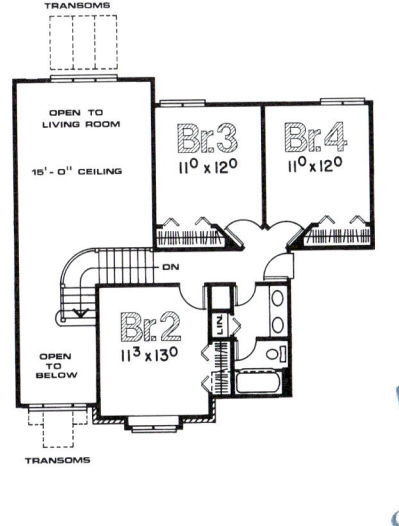

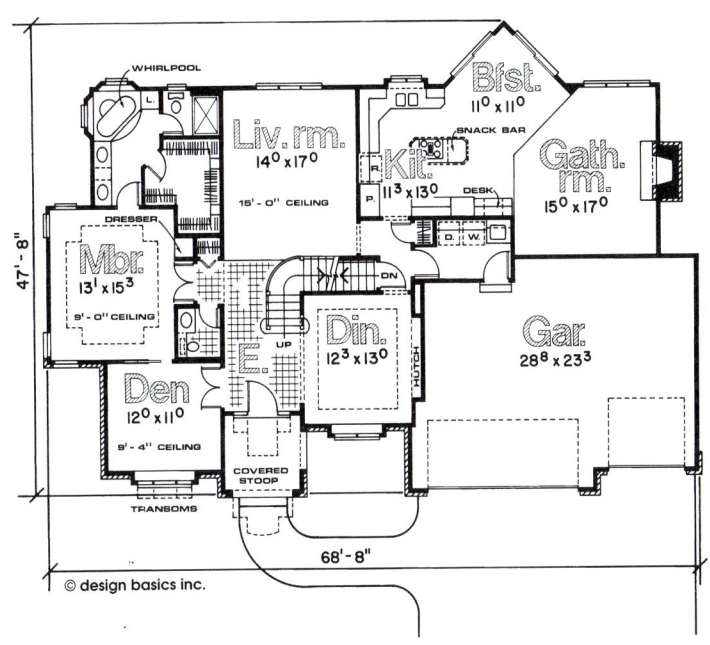

Main: 1829 SQ. FT.
Second: 657 SQ. FT.

Total: 2486 SQ. FT.

ORDER DIRECT - (800) 947-7526 www.designbasics.com 41

complements a magnificent dining room set. The great room is equally impressive with its high ceilings and high windows on the rear wall. Edith says these two rooms work especially well for entertaining. She and Bob recently hosted a group of seventy college students. "The home flowed so easily and nicely," Edith reports. "Everyone's needs were easily accommodated."

Although these areas are possibly the most striking, the couple spends the majority of their time in the kitchen, breakfast area and gathering room. Windows line the rear of the breakfast area and gathering room, filling them with sunshine. On most days, Bob and Edith don't have to turn on any lights because of all the natural light coming in.

During a typical evening you can find them playing a game of Canasta at their card table in the gathering room, or relaxing on the couches. "With the fireplace and the wood floors, it's a very comfortable, warm, relaxing place to be. It's where we live on a daily basis," Edith says.

When their three grown children and their families come to visit, Bob and Edith have plenty of space to accommodate them. "The upper level is nice to have," Edith comments, "because we utilize it when we have company. But when we're alone we can just close it off and live on the main level."

Choosing a home wasn't an easy decision for the two. "I had looked and looked and looked," Edith recalls, "and finally found this and thought it would take care of our needs. Special details like the archways through the entrance of the house and the transom windows in the master bedroom and great room make it very attractive. It's a very hospitable house and easy to keep and enjoy. I'm glad we kept looking; we've been very pleased with this home."

BUILT BY: Sherwood Homes

Northland

#44M- 2322 Price Code 30

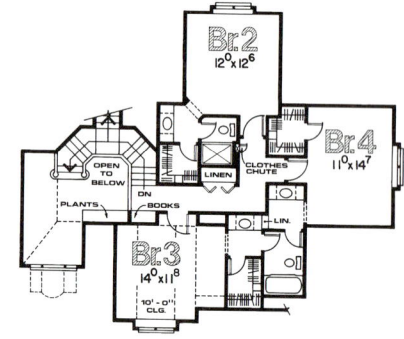

Main: 2169 Sq. Ft.
Second: 898 Sq. Ft.

Total: 3067 Sq. Ft.

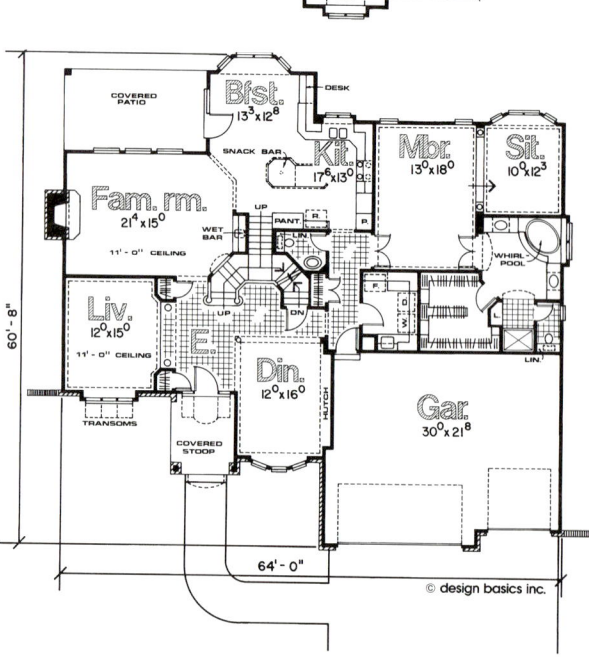

IMPRESSIONS- *Homes & Places for Real People*

Tuxford

#44M-24003   Price Code 17

1762 Finished Sq. Ft.

NOTE: 9 ft. main level walls

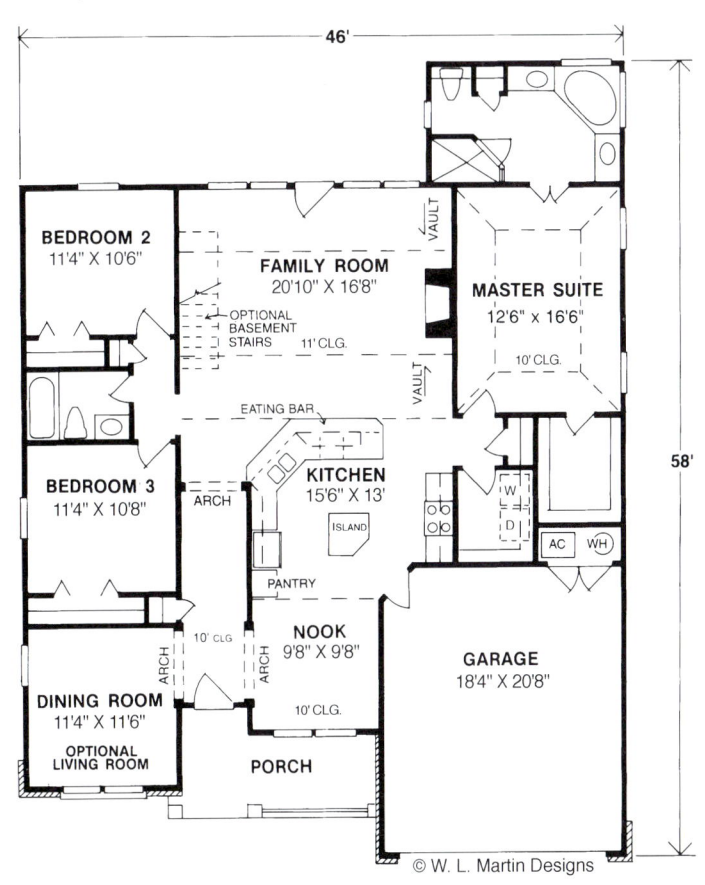

BUILT BY: Grimshaw Builders

© W. L. Martin Designs

BUILT BY: Tweedt Engineering & Construction

This home may have been altered from the plan's original design.

#44M-2414 *Price Code 23*

Stanton

#44M-2618 *Price Code 21*

Paisley

BUILT BY: Unique Homes

This home may have been altered from the plan's original design.

Included in the breakfast area and kitchen are a desk, snack bar and open access to the family room.

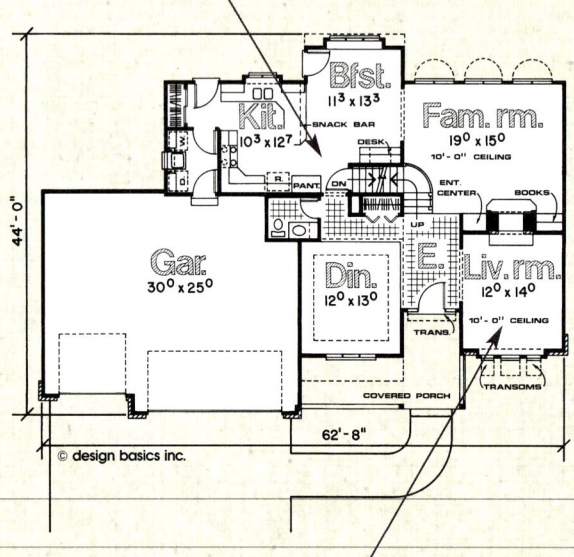

Extra storage space in the garage is an added benefit for home improvement projects.

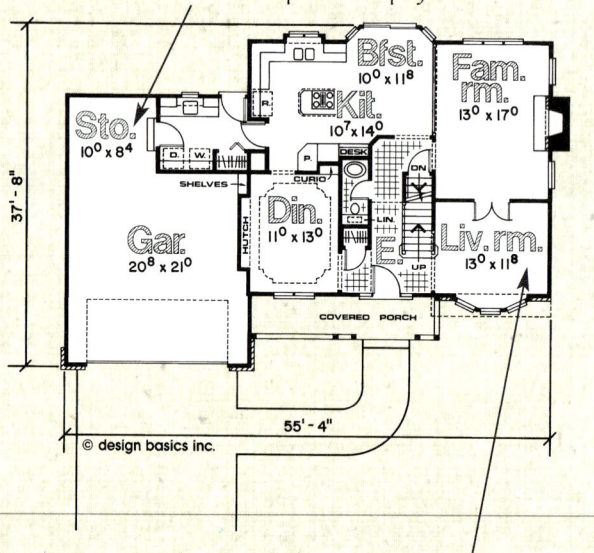

A see-thru fireplace, entertainment center and bookcase will be favorites in the volume family room.

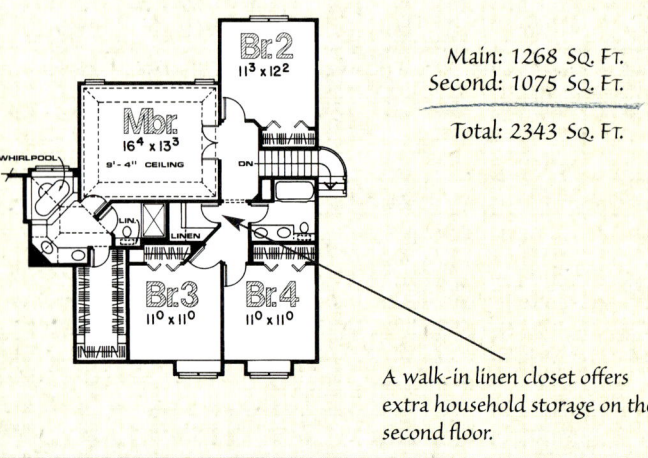

Main: 1268 SQ. FT.
Second: 1075 SQ. FT.

Total: 2343 SQ. FT.

A walk-in linen closet offers extra household storage on the second floor.

French doors expand the living room and family room for large gatherings.

His and her compartments organize the walk-in closet in the master suite.

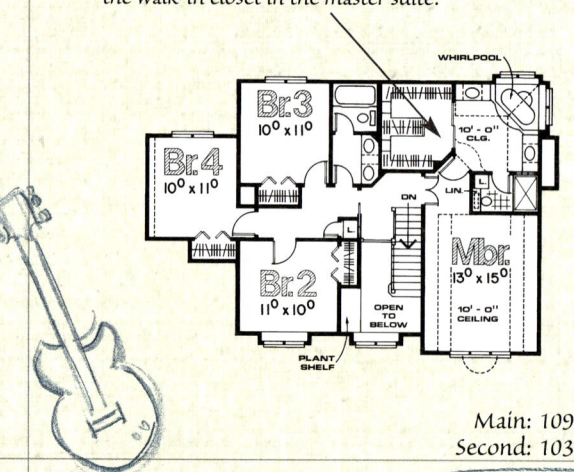

Main: 1093 SQ. FT.
Second: 1038 SQ. FT.

Total: 2131 SQ. FT.

IMPRESSIONS— *Homes & Places for Real People*

BUILT BY: Southern States Construction

Pine Ridge

#44M-8096 *Price Code* 18

This home may have been altered from the plan's original design.

BUILT BY: Miter Construction

This home may have been altered from the plan's original design.

Ambrose

#44M-2701 *Price Code* 23

The spacious kitchen and breakfast area welcome guests from the impressive great room.

Plenty of counter space in the kitchen is beneficial when preparing meals or entertaining casually.

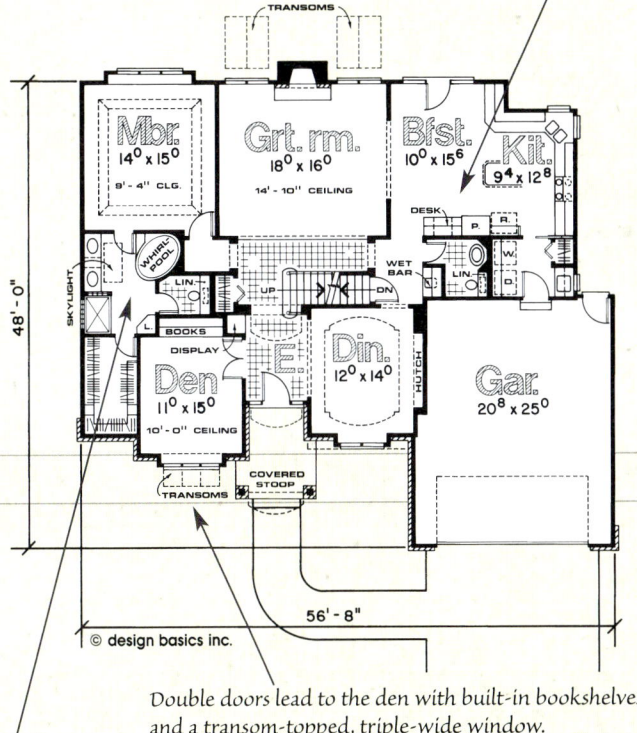

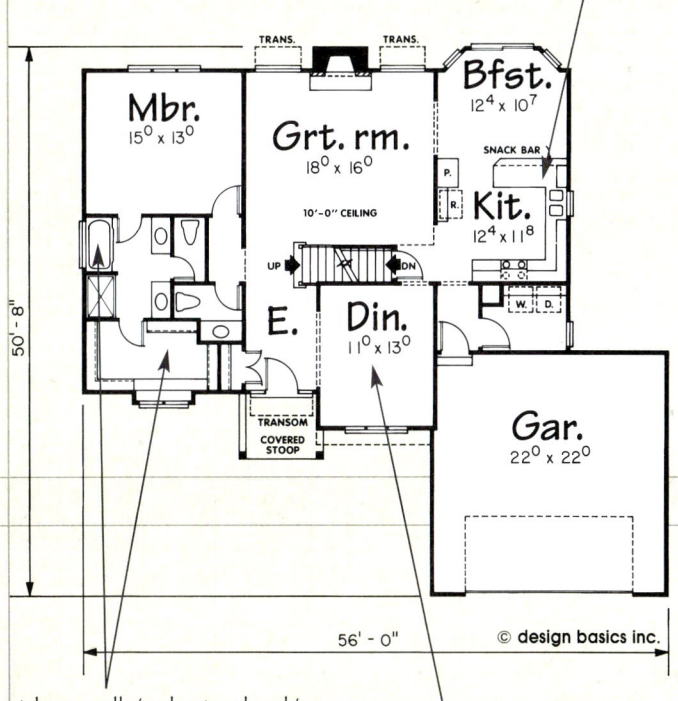

Double doors lead to the den with built-in bookshelves and a transom-topped, triple-wide window.

A large, walk-in closet and soaking tub are amenities in the master suite.

A skylight illuminates the master bath featuring an oval whirlpool and long, walk-in closet.

The formal dining room is strategically placed within steps of the kitchen.

Main: 1701 Sq. Ft.
Second: 639 Sq. Ft.
Total: 2340 Sq. Ft.

Main: 1412 Sq. Ft.
Second: 425 Sq. Ft.
Total: 1837 Sq. Ft.

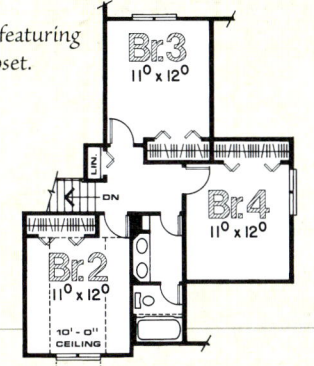

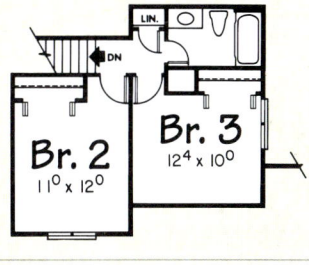

ORDER DIRECT - (800) 947-7526   www.designbasics.com   45

This home may have been altered from the plan's original design.

BUILT BY: Weinandy Construction

#44M-2761 *Price Code* 13

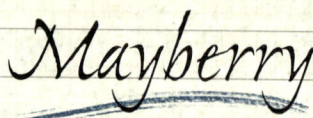
Mayberry

BUILT BY: Mark Hughes Construction

#44M-2723 *Price Code* 26

Armburst

This home may have been altered from the plan's original design.

Functioning as one large living area, the kitchen, hearth room and breakfast area form a central hub for daily activity.

A see-thru fireplace warms both the great room and hearth room.

A three-sided entertainment center caters to an informal lifestyle with viewing capacity from the great room, breakfast area or kitchen.

A sloped ceiling adds interest to the great room and its view to the back.

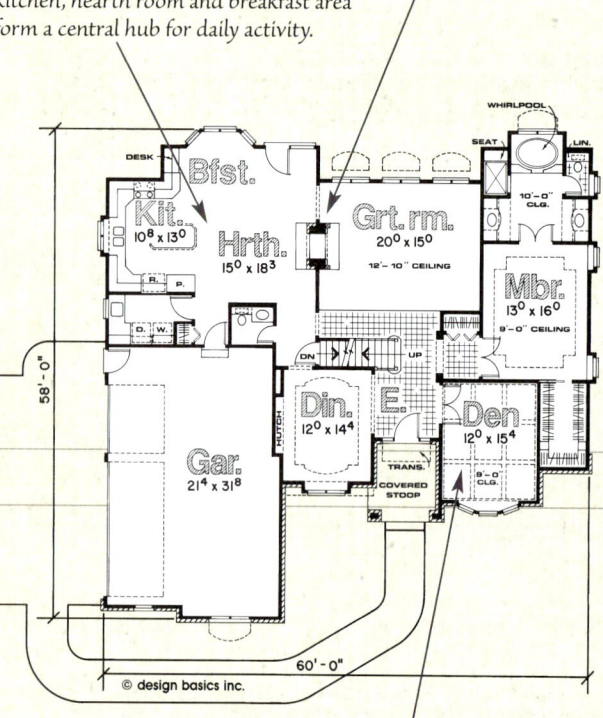

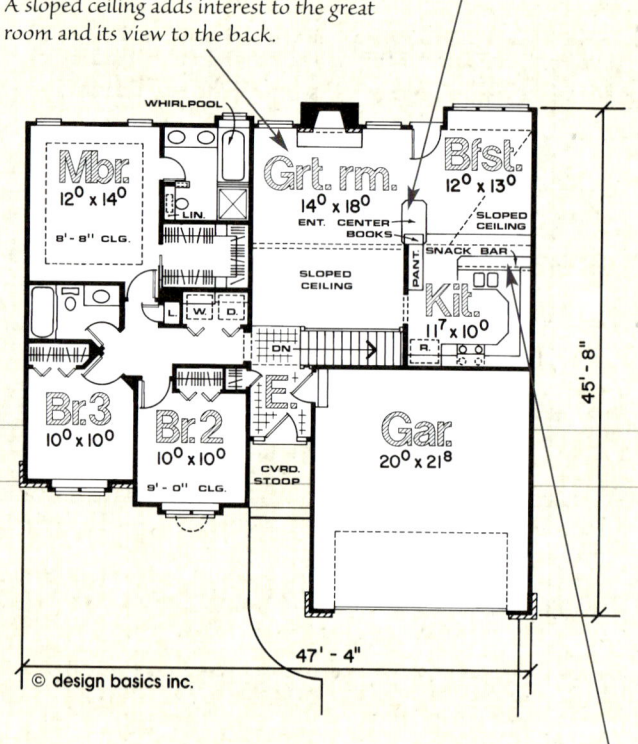

A private den with spider-beam ceiling would be perfect as a home office.

A snack bar in the kitchen makes it easy to serve a quick, casual meal.

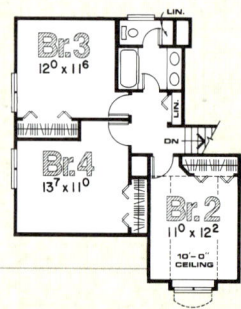

Main: 1972 SQ. FT.
Second: 673 SQ. FT.
Total: 2645 SQ. FT.

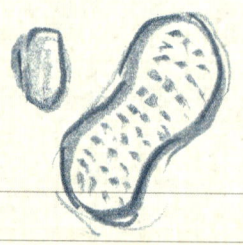

1341 Finished SQ. FT.

IMPRESSIONS— *Homes & Places for Real People*

BUILT BY: Robert Siberneck

This home may have been altered from the plan's original design.

#44M-2800 *Price Code 29* — *Appleton*

#44M-1856 *Price Code 23*

BUILT BY: Buda H0mes Inc.

This home may have been altered from the plan's original design.

This organized kitchen features two islands, one with a huge snack bar and another to shorten trips to the sink and stove.

A cathedral ceiling and tall windows characterize the gathering room, just off the kitchen.

Island kitchen and breakfast area have sunny windows, wrapping counters, desk and pantry.

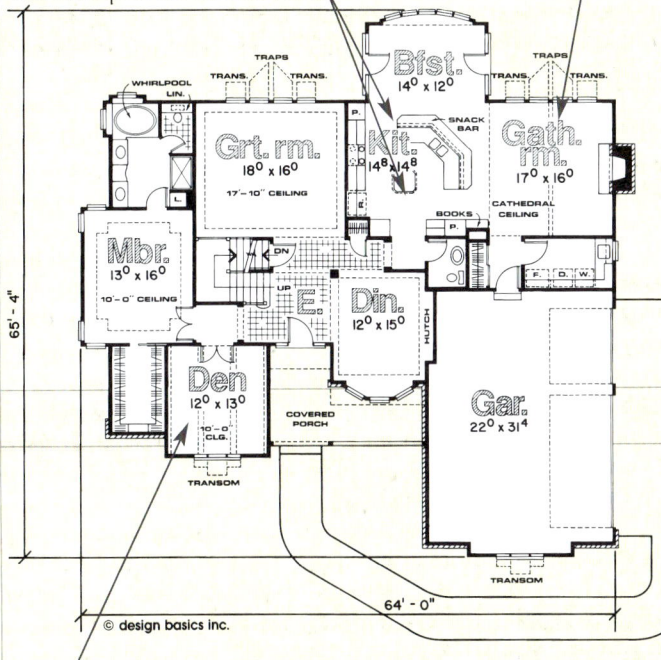

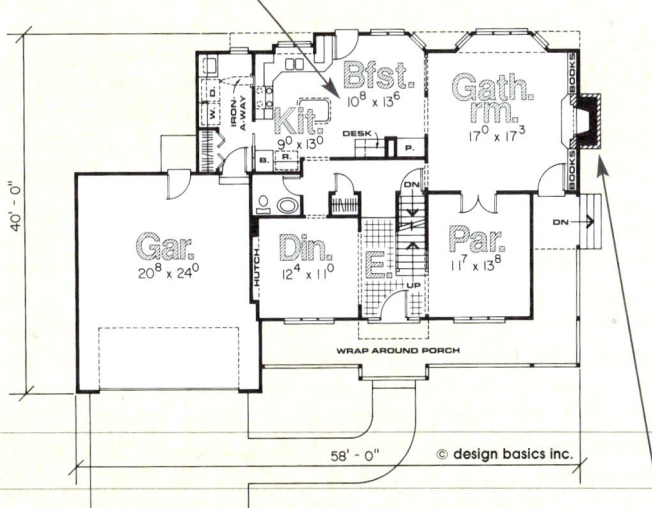

Gathering room has bayed window and fireplace framed by bookcases.

Double doors reveal the den with volume ceiling– perfect for a homework center.

Luxurious master suite features private veranda, compartmented bath, 2-person whirlpool and huge, walk-in closet.

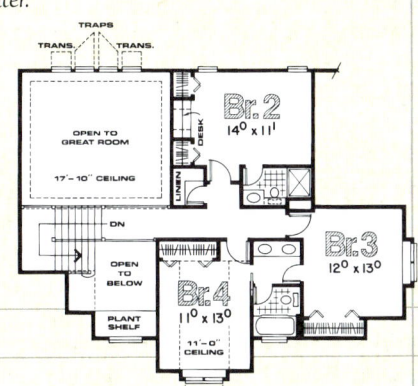

Main: 2158 Sq. Ft.
Second: 821 Sq. Ft.

Total: 2979 Sq. Ft.

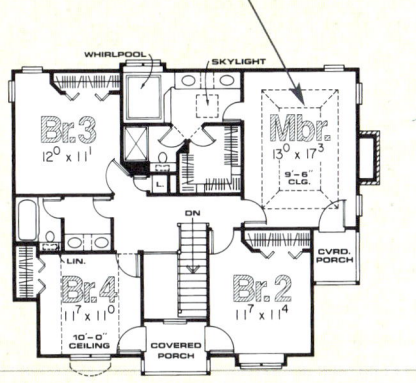

Main: 1188 Sq. Ft.
Second: 1139 Sq. Ft.

Total: 2327 Sq. Ft.

ORDER DIRECT - (800) 947-7526   www.designbasics.com

Design Quality #6

A. The Corinth
B. The Normandy
C. The Hawthorne

Luxurious Comfort

You've sacrificed, worked hard, and done without some things to get where you are. Now it's time to reap the rewards and enjoy the good life— to savor every day delights, take more vacations and stop to smell the roses. You've earned the right to be choosy about where you live, too. Why not pick a home that will pamper your family with grand, spacious rooms... ample cabinets and closets... special amenities to provide extra convenience and comfort... and gorgeous design and details?

3 Views...

A. The Corinth is simply magnificent inside and out. Stately columns divide the family room from the breakfast area. An octagon-shaped sitting room and a see-through fireplace provide added elegance in the master suite. Every bedroom has a walk-in closet. Even the screened porch is stylish with high, sloped ceilings and skylights.

B. A two-story entry with a sweeping staircase and a tall, arched window sets the stage for the Normandy's beautiful floor plan. The open dining room has bowed windows and a special area for a hutch. The great room features a 14-foot-high beamed ceiling, a fireplace, wet bar and transom-topped windows.

C. Special window and ceiling treatments adorn the Hawthorne. The master bedroom and dining room have boxed ceilings while the kitchen, breakfast and gathering room have elaborate sloped ceilings. Bowed windows in the great room and a unique window in the dining room add drama.

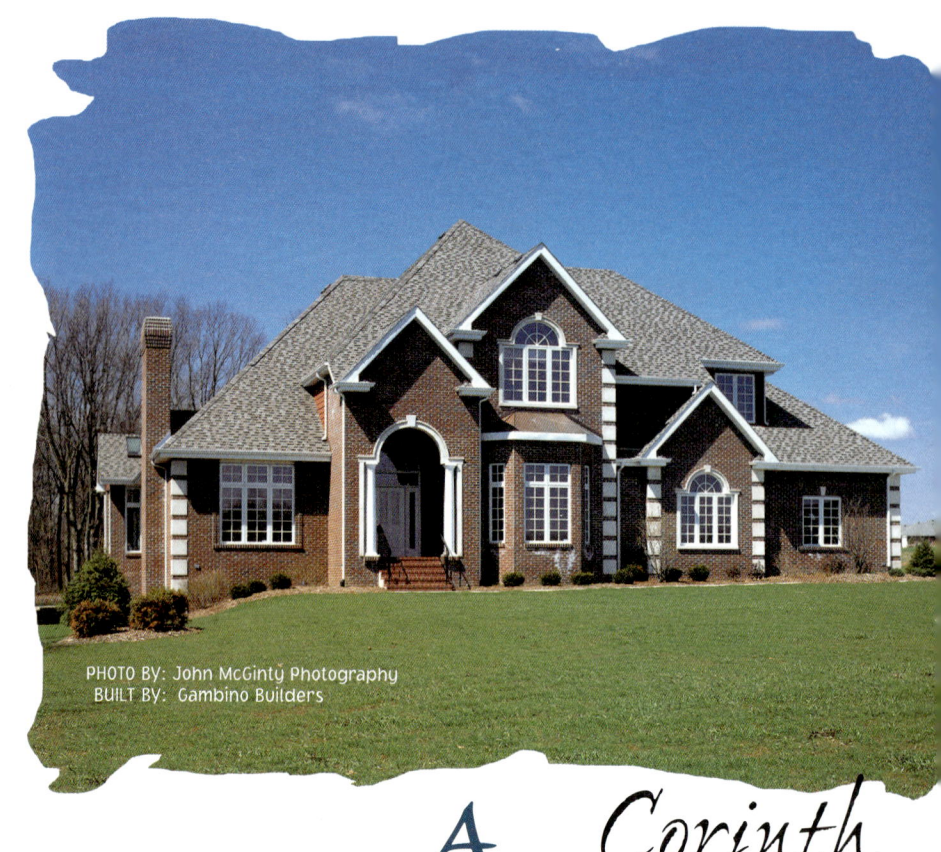

PHOTO BY: John McGinty Photography
BUILT BY: Gambino Builders

A. Corinth

#44M-2332   Price Code 37

Main: 1923 Sq. Ft.
Second: 1852 Sq. Ft.
Total: 3775 Sq. Ft.

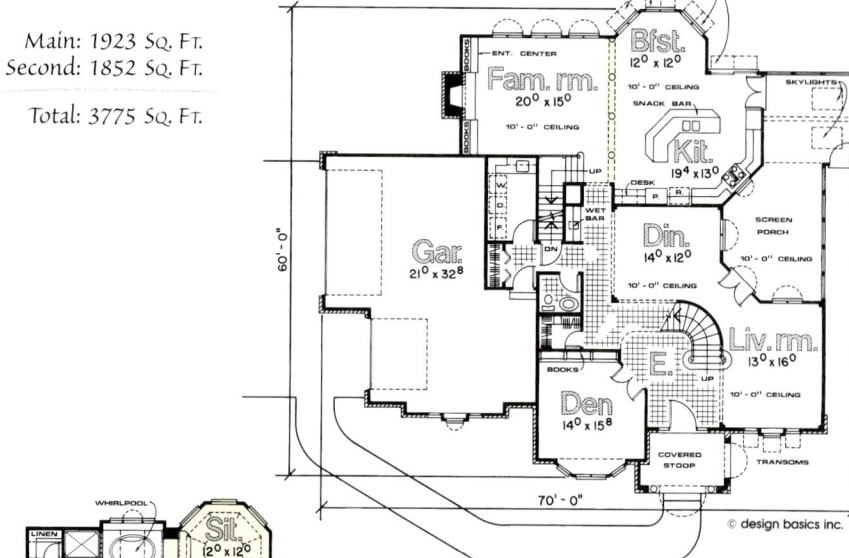

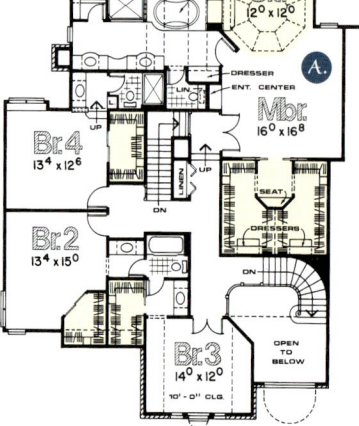

IMPRESSIONS— *Homes & Places for Real People*

BUILT BY: Macfarlane Homebuilders, Inc.

B. Normandy

#44M-2249   *Price Code 31*

Main: 2252 Sq. Ft.
Second: 920 Sq. Ft.

Total: 3172 Sq. Ft.

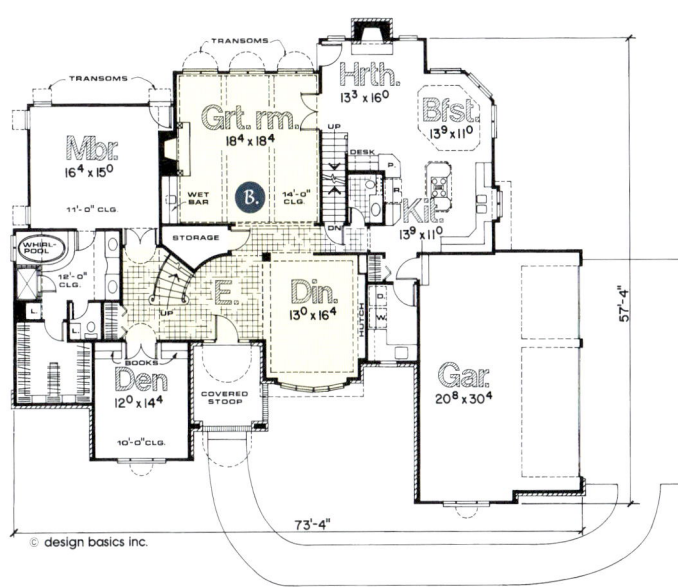

ORDER DIRECT — (800) 947-7526   www.designbasics.com

C. Hawthorne

#44M-2799   Price Code 18

1887 Finished SQ. FT.

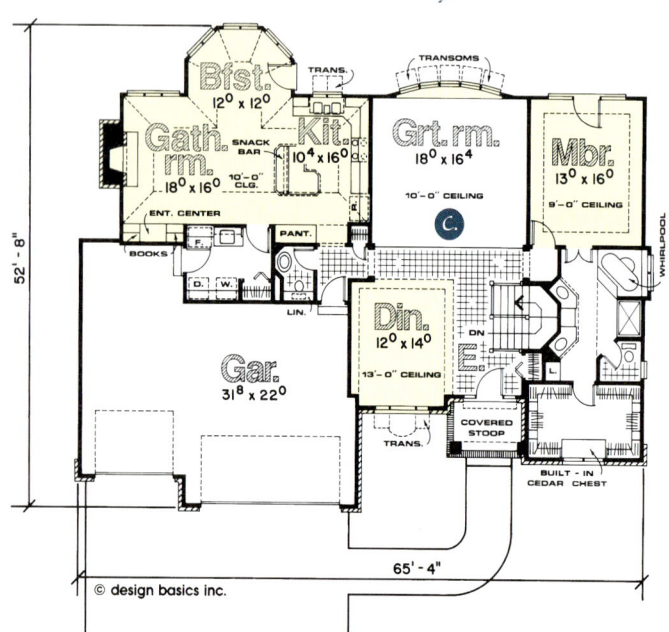

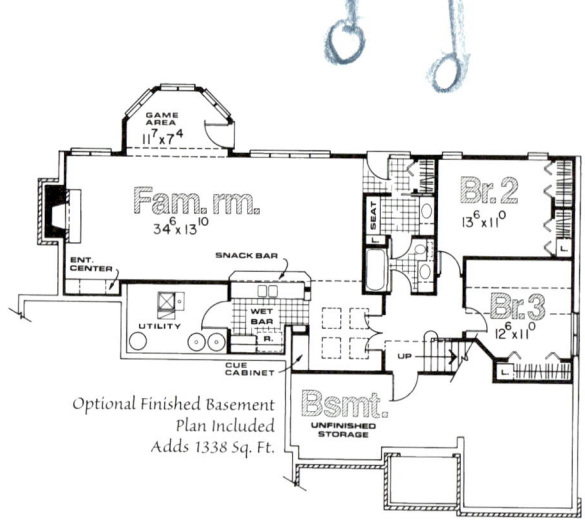

Optional Finished Basement Plan Included
Adds 1338 Sq. Ft.

BUILT BY: Landmark Homes

IMPRESSIONS— *Homes & Places for Real People*

BUILT BY: Benchmark Custom Homes

This home may have been altered from the plan's original design.

#44M-3381 *Price Code 20*

Amanda

Pampering amenities in the master suite include large, bayed windows, special ceiling details, his and her closets, dual lavs and a corner whirlpool tub.

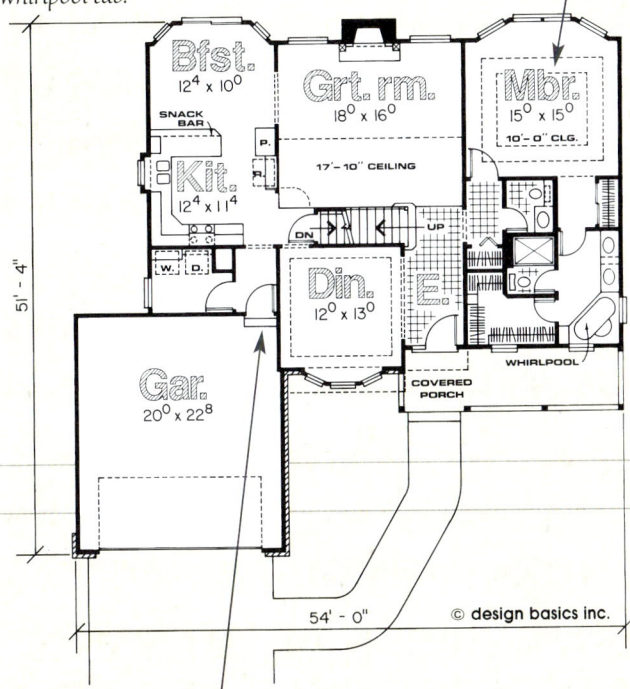

Groceries are carried directly from the garage to the kitchen in a few short steps.

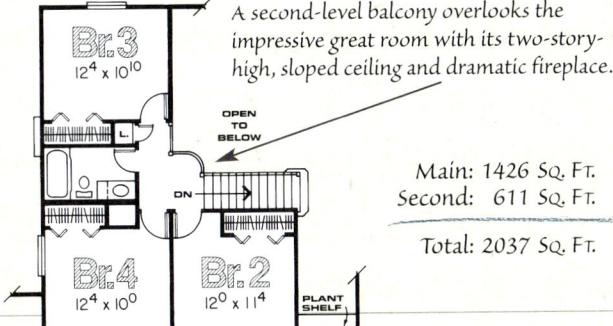

A second-level balcony overlooks the impressive great room with its two-story-high, sloped ceiling and dramatic fireplace.

Main: 1426 Sq. Ft.
Second: 611 Sq. Ft.

Total: 2037 Sq. Ft.

#44M-2619 *Price Code 19*

Oakbrook

BUILT BY: RLR Construction

This home may have been altered from the plan's original design.

The kitchen offers the organization of an island cooktop.

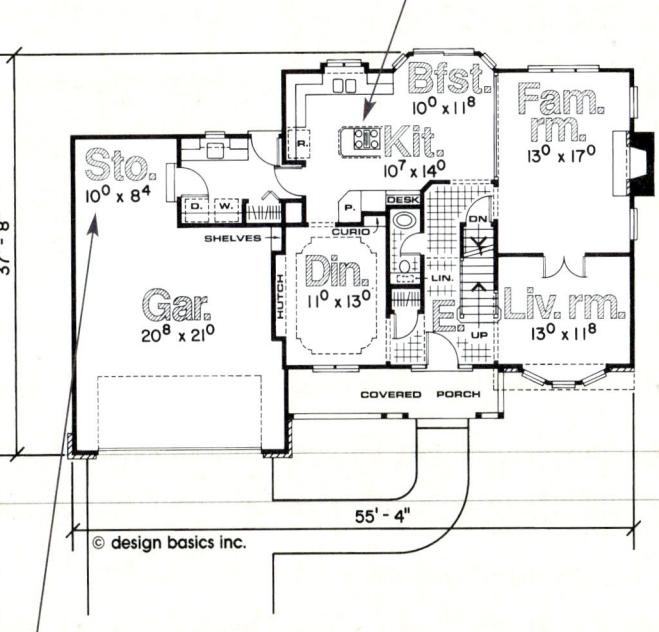

Extra storage space in the garage is perfect for lawn equipment.

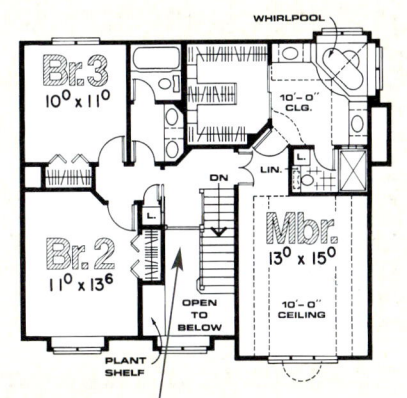

A second-floor balcony overlooks the entry with plant shelf.

Main: 1093 Sq. Ft.
Second: 905 Sq. Ft.

Total: 1998 Sq. Ft.

ORDER DIRECT — (800) 947-7526   www.designbasics.com

Southwest

A gallery of vista and sky: Wide open spaces. Endless sunshine. Wrinkled sandstone hills. Ancient canyons. Cathedrals of rock—masterpieces of natural sculpture. Shifting desert sands in a kaleidoscope of colors. Awe-inspiring mountains covered with ponderosa pines. Lanky palms swaying in the breeze. Turquoise colored sage. Mesquite groves. A clump of prickly pear cactuses. Ancient ruins of past civilizations. An old Spanish mission. A skyline of modern skyscrapers.

A land of legends: Kit Carson, Geronimo, Wyatt Earp, Billy the Kid. Where the spirit of the West lives on: In its peoples' proud independence, fierce determination and informal friendliness. In neighbors who circle their wagons and band together in time of trouble. On large ranches where modern-day cowboys still herd cattle on horseback. At backyard barbecues, spirited chili cook-offs, colorful fiestas and rousing rodeos.

Like Gold Rush days of the past, people are streaming to Southwestern cities... Where memories of winter fade, allergies disappear and breakfast is on a grapefruit tree in the front yard. These city slickers decorate their homes with hand-woven Indian rugs and blankets, chile pepper wreaths, coiled baskets and bright pottery.

They listen to Mexican mariachi bands and open air opera... watch armadillo races and browse art galleries... enjoy Indian ceremonial dances, line dancing and ballet... eat steak and potatoes, pizza and pasta, grilled quail, hominy, fry bread and incendiary salsa. For the threads of many cultures make the Southwest's people as diverse as its landscape.

Design Quality #7

A. The Bancroft
B. The Caldera
C. The Arant

BUILT BY: Tweedt Engineering & Construction

A. Bancroft

#44M-1559   *Price Code* 18

1808 Finished SQ. FT.

SOUTHWESTERN INFORMALITY

Perhaps you're the type who drinks coffee in homey mugs and prefers plain cooking to fancy, gourmet dishes... Who travels light, goes with the flow and encourages guests to make themselves at home. After being prim and proper all day at work, you can't wait to come home, kick your shoes off, slip into your favorite, faded jeans and plop into an overstuffed chair. People who think life is too short to sweat the details will appreciate these informal, no-fuss floor plans. Because home should be a relaxing, comfortable place.

3 VIEWS...

A. Rooms that make for friendly get-togethers are all side by side in the Bancroft. A see-through fireplace and a wet bar connect the kitchen and breakfast area to a spacious great room with ten-foot ceilings. A roomy snack bar in the kitchen provides a great place to grab a quick bite or to spread out a buffet for guests.

B. A simple floor plan sets a carefree tone in the Caldera. A roomy kitchen with a snack bar and adjoining breakfast area offers ample room for everyday meals. An open dining room at the rear of the home joins the breakfast area and great room for casual entertaining.

C. The Arant has the perfect floor plan for casual gatherings. A see-thru fireplace connects a large great room to a very open kitchen, breakfast and hearth area. The dining room in the front of the home could also be converted to a den.

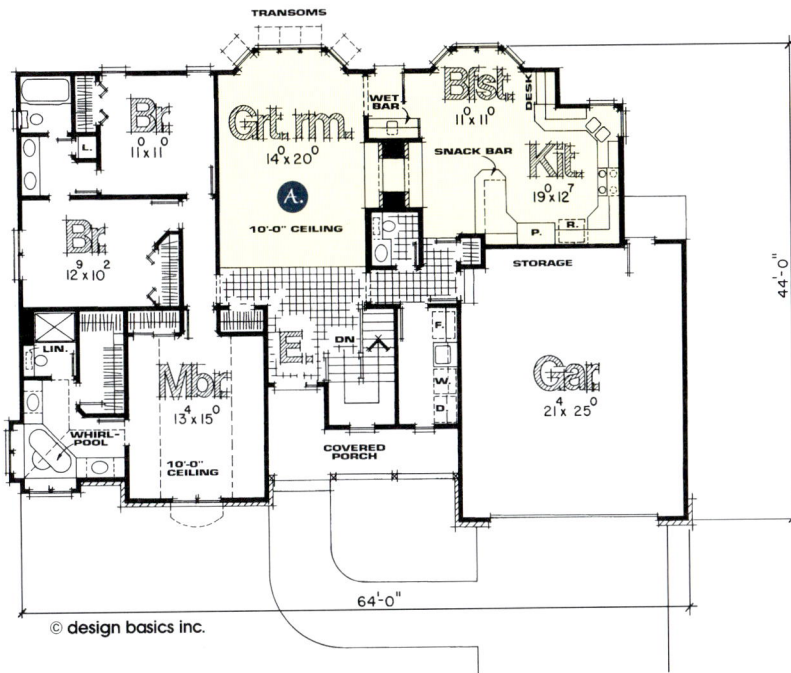

ORDER DIRECT - (800) 947-7526   www.designbasics.com

B. Caldera

#44M-4952 Price Code 21

Main: 1008 Sq. Ft.
Second: 1136 Sq. Ft.

Total: 2144 Sq. Ft.

NOTE: 9 ft. main level walls

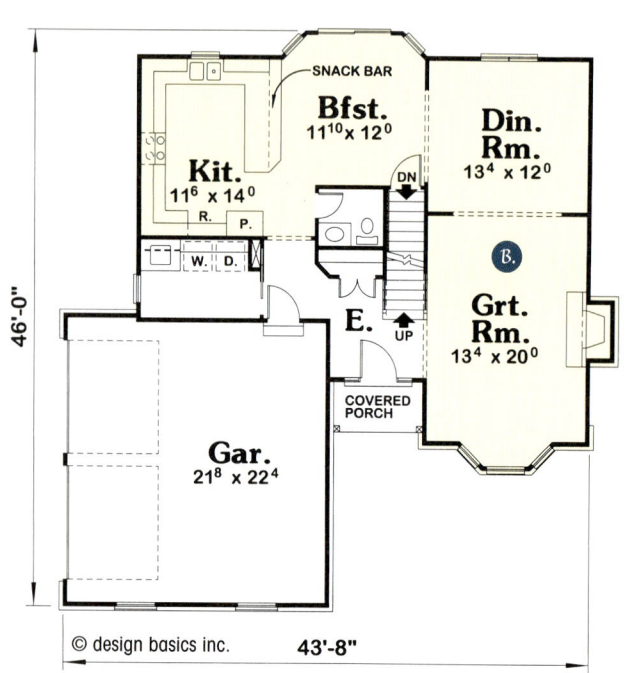

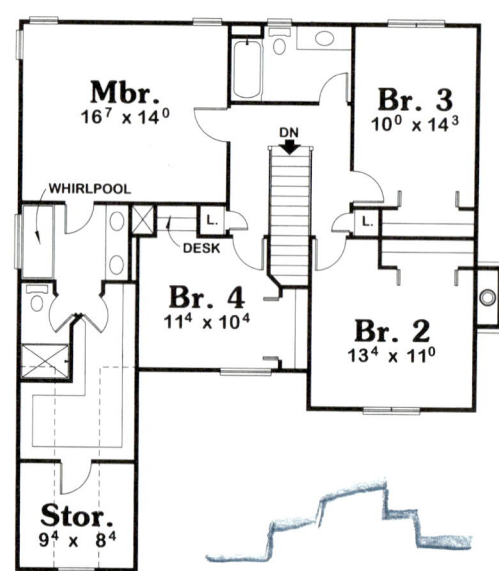

IMPRESSIONS - *Homes & Places for Real People*

C. Arant

#44M-2261 *Price Code 24*

Main: 1733 Sq. Ft.
Second: 672 Sq. Ft.

Total: 2405 Sq. Ft.

BUILT BY: Webb Building & Development

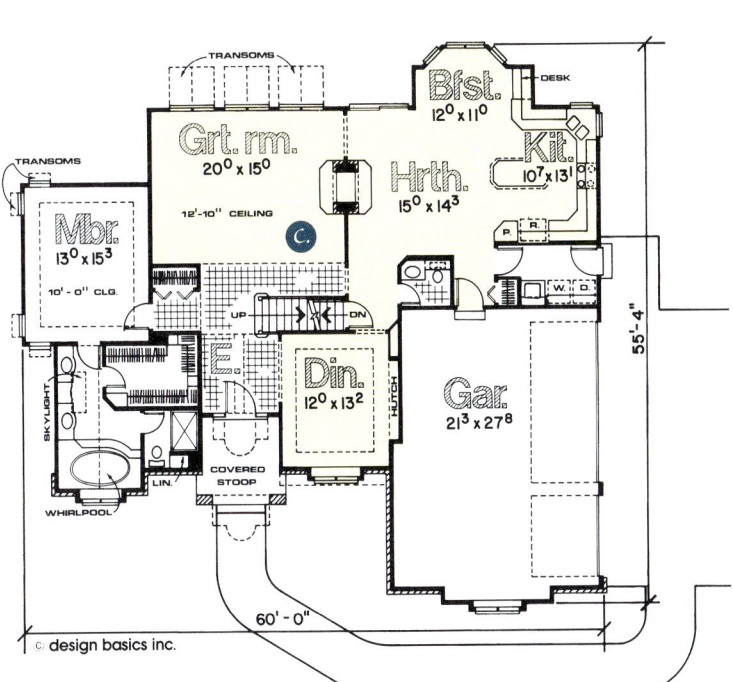
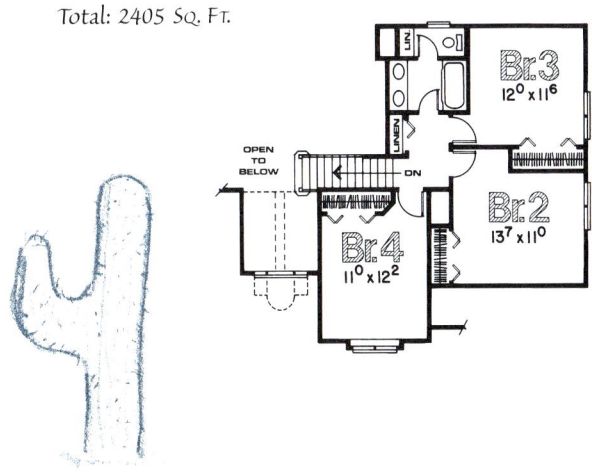

Home Owner Impressions

on Living in the Prairie

BUILT BY: Sudon Brothers Inc.

A deliberate job search brought Susan, Dave and their three teenage children to Arizona two years ago. They lived in Ohio at the time, but were attracted to the state's nature, sunshine and year-round outdoor activities. After Dave found a position, the search for a suitable home began. Susan and Dave looked through thirty homes during a long weekend, but couldn't find anything they were comfortable with.

Dave resumed the search two weeks later when he came back for some business meetings. His realtor showed him a house in a new development surrounded by woods and hillsides. It didn't appeal to Dave, but the home across the street, Design Basics' "Prairie," did. Dave walked inside the Prairie and fell in love with it. He immediately called Susan. She responded without hesitating, "If you like it that much, I'm sure I'm going to like it." So Dave bought the house— sight unseen on the part of his trusting wife.

When she finally saw her new home, Susan knew she "was going to love it" before she got out of the car. She explains, "It has a very nice, long porch on the front and sort of a traditional, yet modern look."

There have been no regrets in the two years since. "I love the house; it has everything we were looking for," Susan says simply. The Prairie suits the family's busy lifestyle. Dave is a corporate senior vice-president. Susan is a registered nurse who contours her career around her children's schedules.

continued on page 58

Prairie

#44M- 2285   *Price Code* 21

Main: 1505 Sq. Ft.
Second: 610 Sq. Ft.

Total: 2115 Sq. Ft.

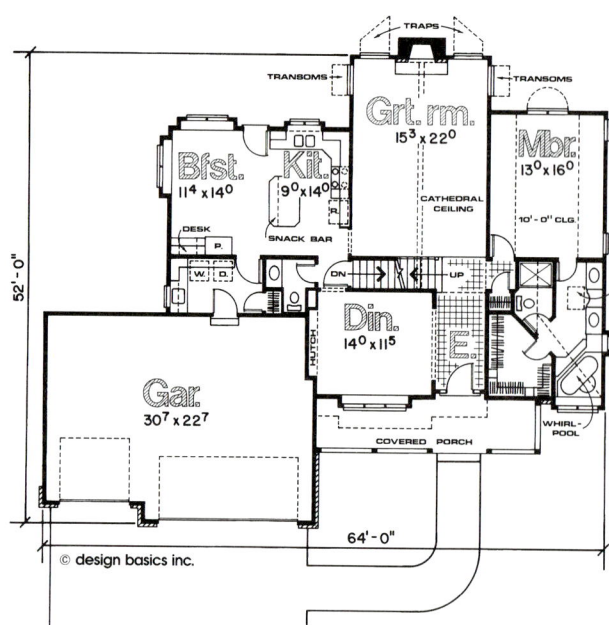

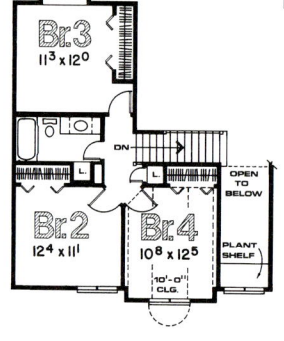

Rose Hollow

#44M-8108   Price Code 17

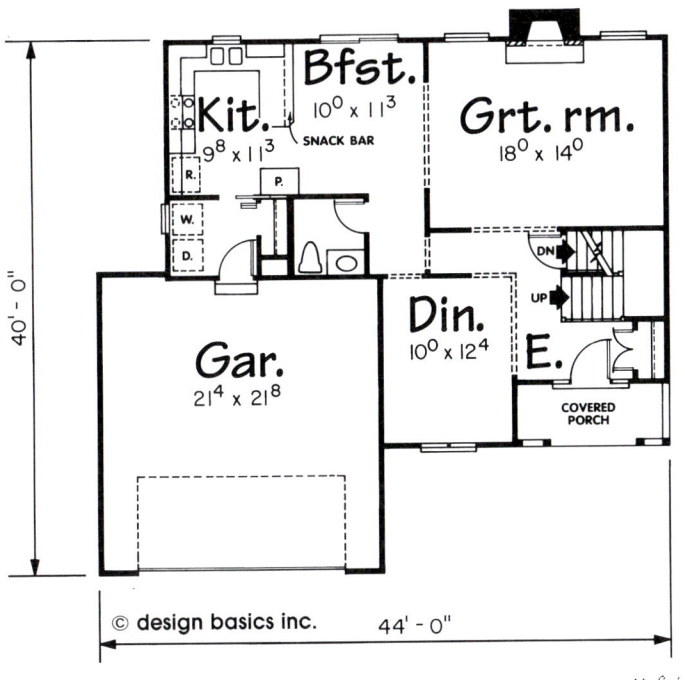

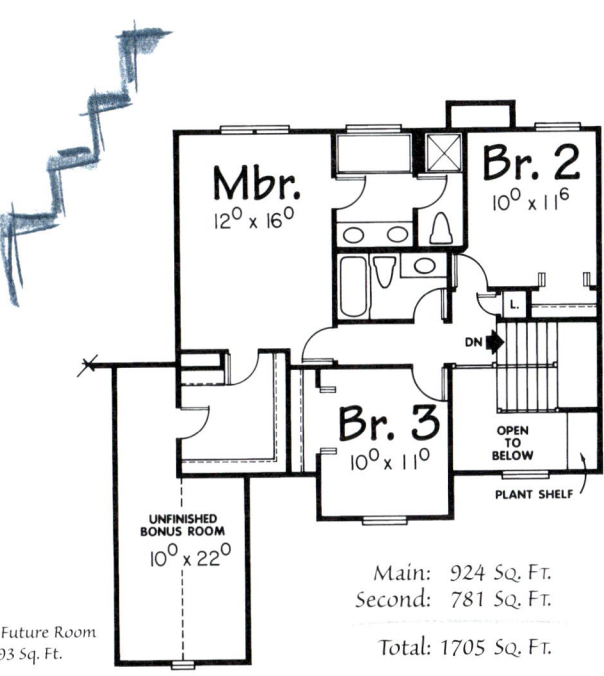

Unfinished Future Room adds 193 Sq. Ft.

Main: 924 Sq. Ft.
Second: 781 Sq. Ft.

Total: 1705 Sq. Ft.

BUILT BY: Premier Builders

ORDER DIRECT - (800) 947-7526   www.designbasics.com

Because houses in their area don't have basements, the Prairie's three-car garage, ample closets, and abundant storage are very important. "I still have an empty cupboard in my kitchen," Susan boasts, "because the pantry area is so big."

"The home is very free-feeling inside," she continues, "and yet there is private space. The family room can be completely closed off– which is nice when someone wants to watch a movie. I love the kitchen; it's very big and open and I can be in there getting a meal ready while my son works on homework in the dining room."

Susan loves entertaining: "This house is ideal for it. The kitchen and great room are so open– with only a snack bar in between. We're able to open the entire area, with people mingling in the great room, the dining room and the kitchen."

With its high ceilings and windows, the great room may be the family's favorite area. The home backs onto a wood filled with pine and oak trees and the room's large windows seem to bring the natural beauty inside. At night they can sit and watch the stars.

Susan credits the builder with doing a wonderful job of choosing colors and putting on the right finishing touches. The cabinets are light oak; the woodwork is painted in a very light, cream color. He gave the home a Southwestern look by rounding all the corners on doors and openings between the rooms and giving the walls a slightly rough texture.

Just as the family has no regrets about their home, they are also highly pleased with their new locale. They live in the cooler part of Arizona where summer temperatures rarely pass the 80's and there's always a breeze. "We spend a lot more time outdoors here because the sun is almost always out," Susan comments. "In the winter the snow is beautiful. By afternoon it's warmed up enough to feel warm and the snow melts off the streets. It's just really a nice place to live."

BUILT BY: E&G Construction

Fenton

#44M-2100 *Price Code* 18

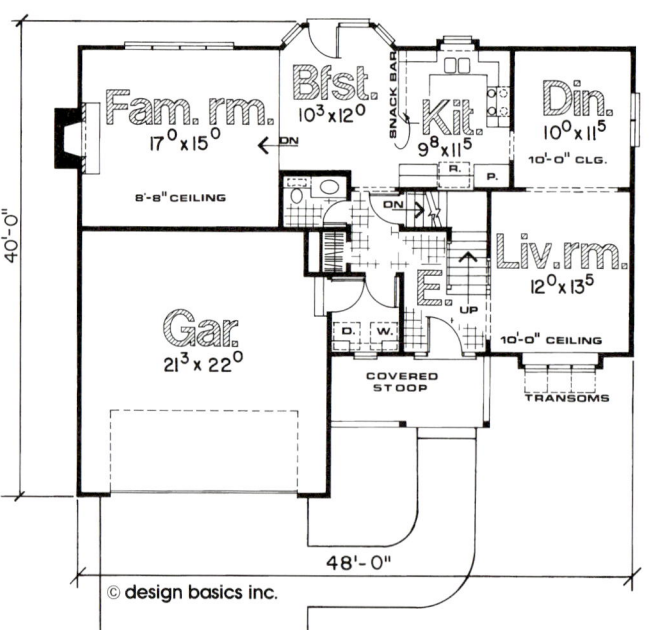

Main: 1042 SQ. FT.
Second: 803 SQ. FT.

Total: 1845 SQ. FT.

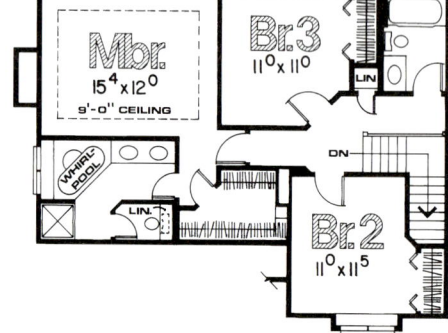

Meadowview Manor

#44M-9114   Price Code 41

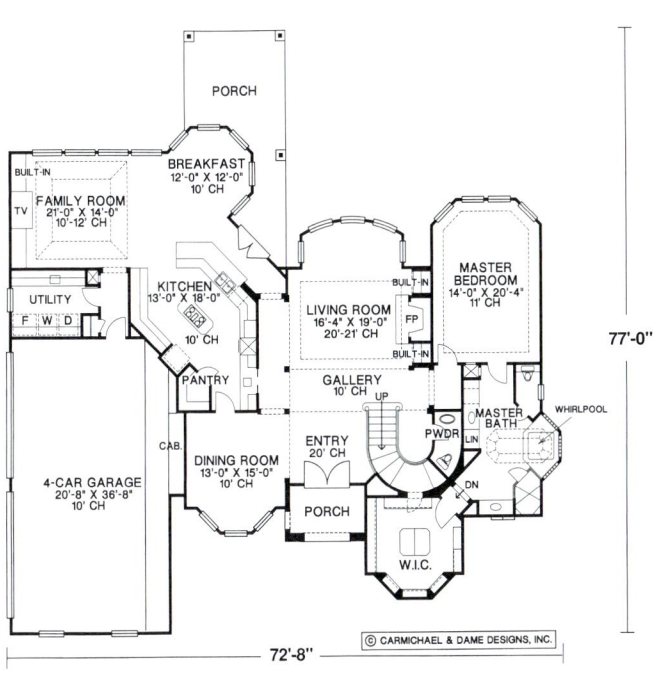

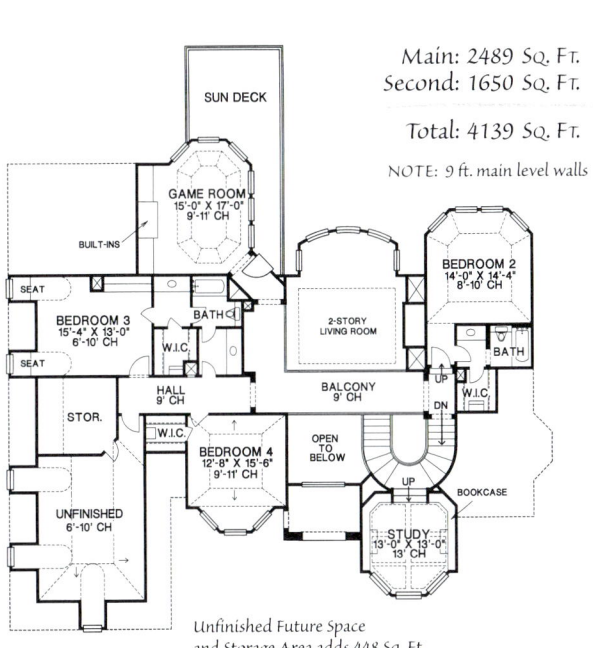

Main: 2489 Sq. Ft.
Second: 1650 Sq. Ft.

Total: 4139 Sq. Ft.

NOTE: 9 ft. main level walls

Unfinished Future Space
and Storage Area adds 448 Sq. Ft.

ORDER DIRECT – (800) 947-7526   www.designbasics.com   59

BUILT BY: Quail Valley Homes

This home may have been altered from the plan's original design.

Rollins

#44M-2894 Price Code 26

The master suite features access to a private covered porch – a great place to get away.

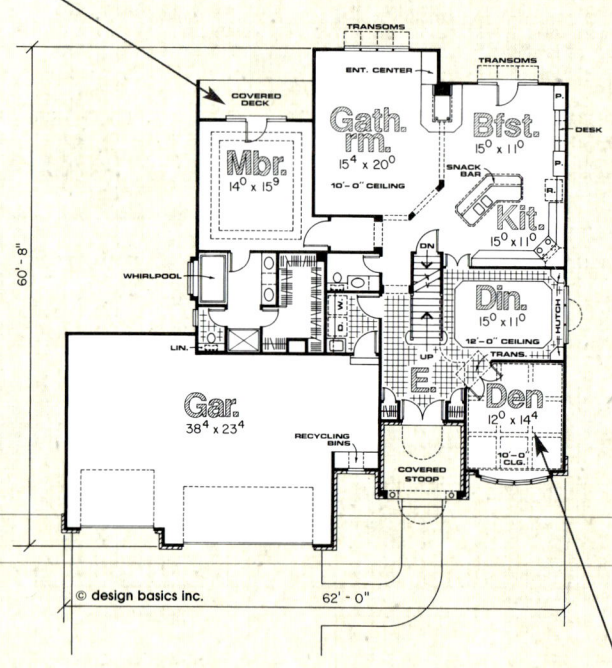

A spider-beamed ceiling and double doors highlight the den.

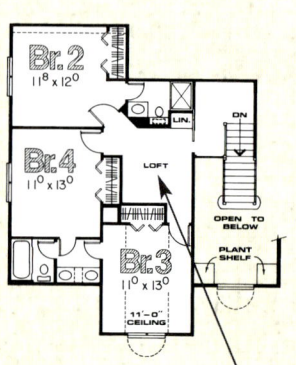

Main: 1800 SQ. FT.
Second: 803 SQ. FT.

Total: 2603 SQ. FT.

A second-floor loft is a great place for a homework area and the home computer.

Norwick

#44M-2650 Price Code 24

BUILT BY: RLR Construction

This home may have been altered from the plan's original design.

Spacious family room is complemented by a charming seat next to a bayed window.

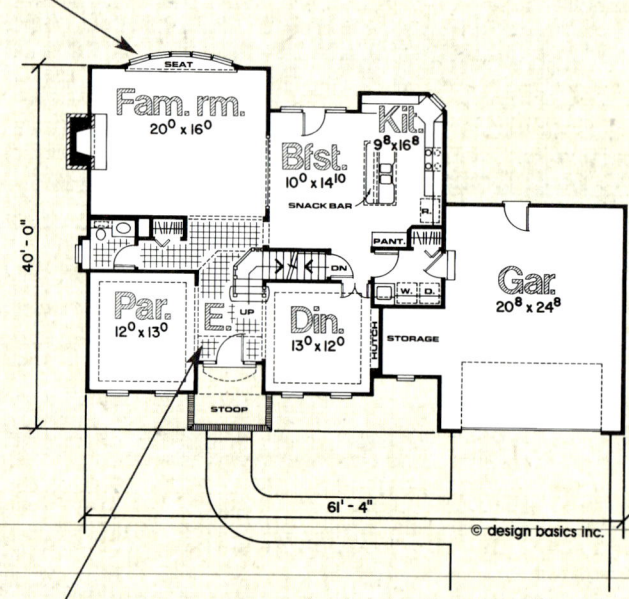

Wide entry with an extra-high ceiling offers a commanding view of the parlor, dining room and family room.

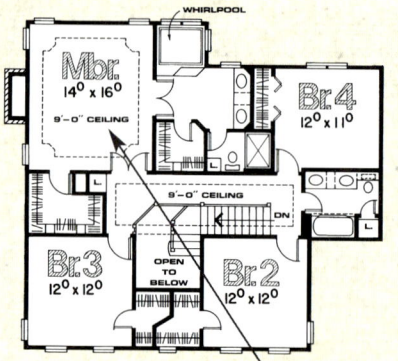

Main: 1294 SQ. FT.
Second: 1187 SQ. FT.

Total: 2481 SQ. FT.

Double doors open to a gorgeous master suite with boxed ceiling, large whirlpool, compartmented bath and his and her walk-in closets.

IMPRESSIONS— *Homes & Places for Real People*

BUILT BY: RLR Construction

This home may have been altered from the plan's original design.

#44M-3006 *Price Code* 18

Grayson

#44M-3063 *Price Code* 19

BUILT BY: Glenwood Contracting

Taylor

This home may have been altered from the plan's original design.

The island kitchen boasts a pantry and plenty of counter space.

Tall windows on either side of the fireplace offer a welcoming atmosphere in the family room.

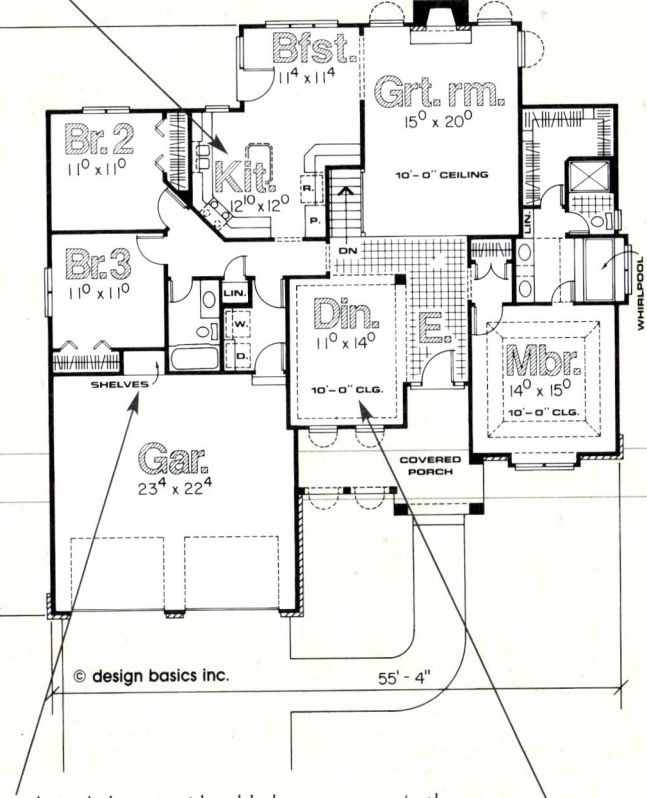

Storage space in the garage leaves room for bikes, lawn mowers, and other equipment.

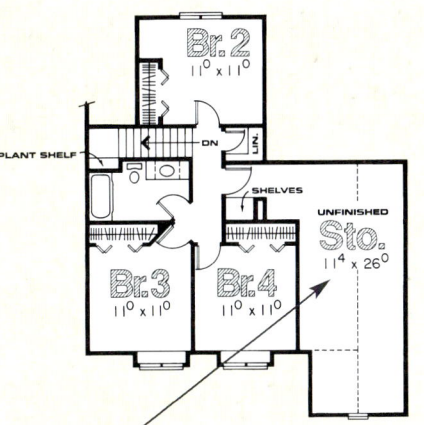

Main: 1348 Sq. Ft.
Second: 609 Sq. Ft.

Total: 1957 Sq. Ft.

Unfinished Future Room Adds 351 Sq. Ft.

Built-in shelves provide added storage space in the garage.

The formal dining room is graced by tiered ceiling and expansive views to the great room.

1806 Finished Sq. Ft.

Three bedrooms share the second floor with a massive storage room offering the potential for a studio.

ORDER DIRECT – (800) 947-7526   www.designbasics.com

BUILT BY: Tweedt Engineering & Construction

This home may have been altered from the plan's original design.

#44M-3064 *Price Code* 20

Eldridge

- A 10-foot ceiling adds volume to the master bath.
- An island counter helps organize the kitchen.

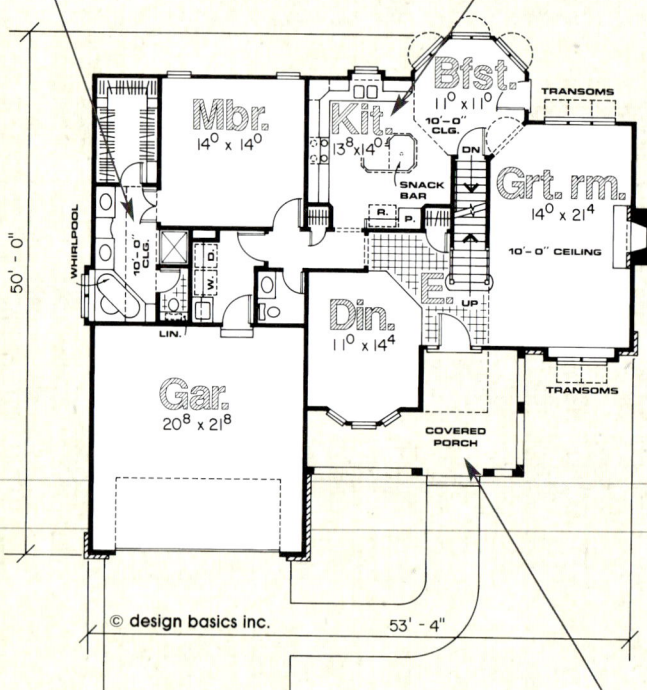

A large porch welcomes the addition of a comfortable bench.

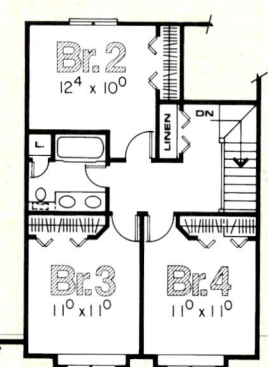

Main: 1414 SQ. FT.
Second: 641 SQ. FT.
Total: 2055 SQ. FT.

#44M-3010 *Price Code* 14

Quimby

BUILT BY: Tweedt Engineering & Construction

This home may have been altered from the plan's original design.

- Enjoy breakfast in the bright dinette or in the great outdoors on the rear covered porch.
- Dual arched openings between the kitchen and dining room are highlighted by built-in bookcases.

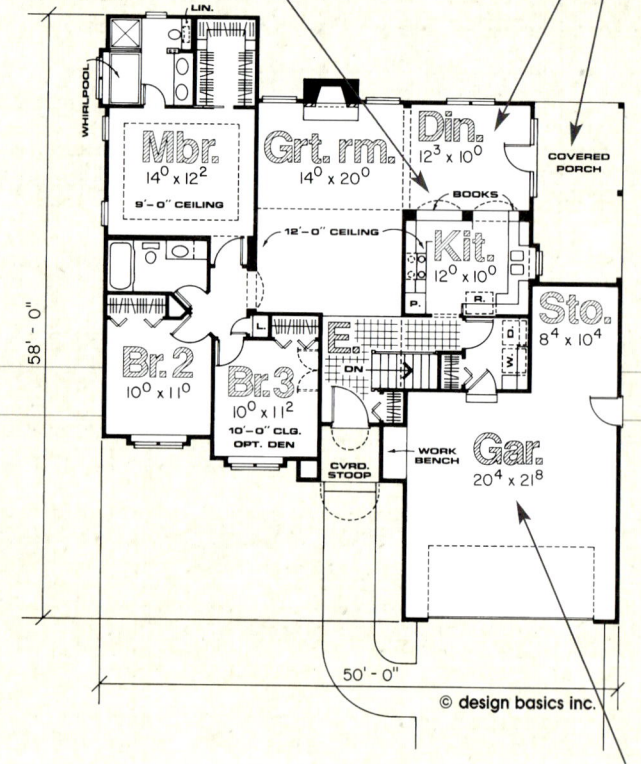

The well-planned garage offers ample storage space and a built-in work bench.

1422 Finished SQ. FT.

---

62   IMPRESSIONS— *Homes & Places for Real People*

BUILT BY: Blake Homes

This home may have been altered from the plan's original design.

Torrey

#44M-3096 *Price Code* 17

The island kitchen with snack bar features plenty of light from the breakfast area and an angled window above the sink.

Many windows line the rear of the home, offering excellent views.

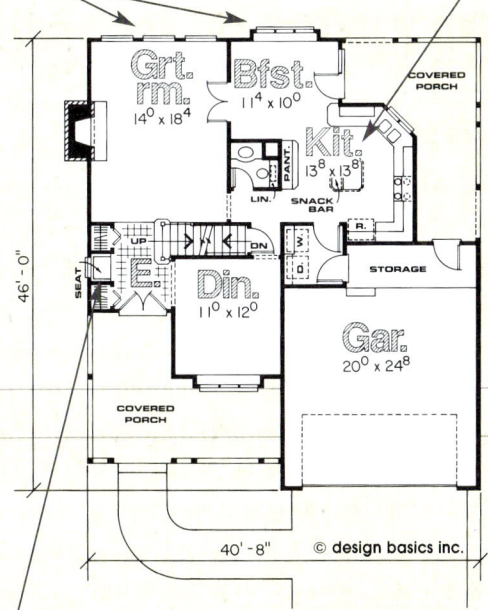

A window seat brings a sense of nostalgia to the front entry.

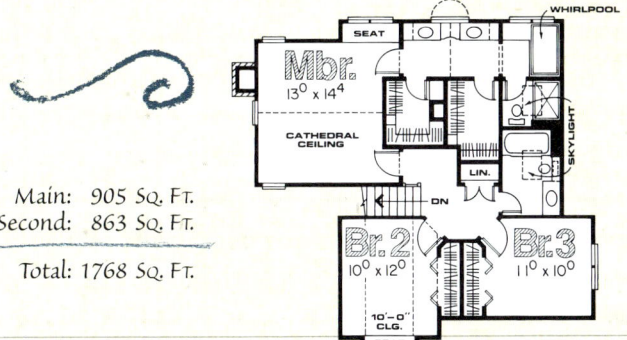

Main: 905 Sq. Ft.
Second: 863 Sq. Ft.
Total: 1768 Sq. Ft.

#44M-3577 *Price Code* 17

BUILT BY: Benne Builders

This home may have been altered from the plan's original design.

The tempting hearth room is warmed by a fireplace.

A sunny breakfast area has access to the back to go walking or to do yard work.

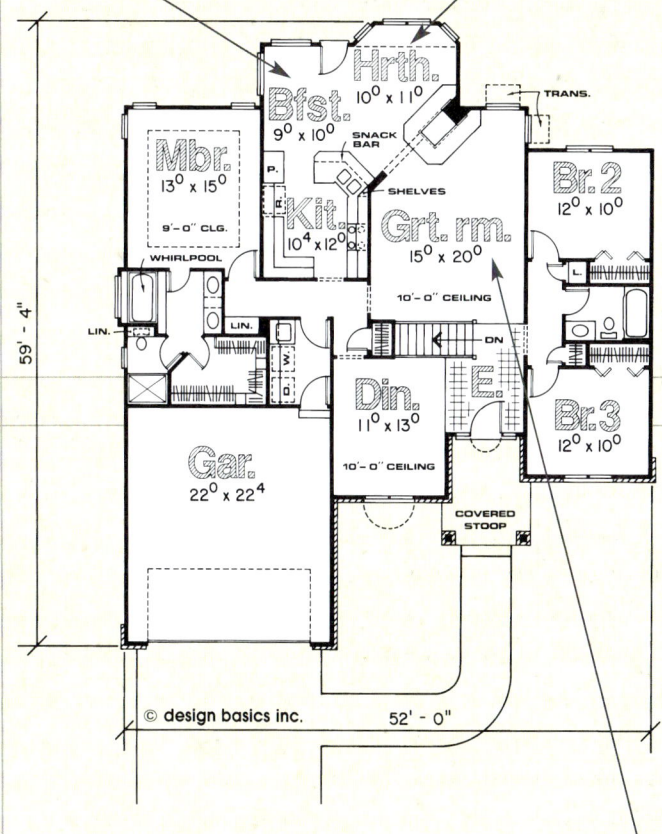

A volume ceiling adds a sense of spaciousness to the great room.

1782 Finished Sq. Ft.

ORDER DIRECT – (800) 947-7526   www.designbasics.com   63

Design Quality #8

A. The Sierra
B. The Newberry
C. The Plainview

BUILT BY: Regal Building Systems

Abundant Sunshine...

There's nothing like being outdoors when the sky is clear blue and the leaves are emerald green. A sunny day seems to brighten your outlook and warm your spirit. And the broad horizons make problems seem smaller. When you can't be outside, the next best thing is having a home with lots of big windows – to make rooms light and airy and bring the great outdoors inside. Imagine watching a bird build a nest, the sun go down in a blaze of glory or the stars come out – all while sitting in the comfort of your own home.

3 Views...

A. The Sierra lets the sun shine in with a row of windows topped with transoms in the great room and breakfast area. Transom-topped windows are also featured in the master bedroom and bath. And the two-story entry is flooded with natural light.

B. A sun room fills the kitchen and breakfast area of the Newberry with light, while the family room is brightened by large windows on two walls. Even the garage is sunny with three good-sized windows. A large, wrap-around, covered porch is an added bonus.

C. An abundance of windows in the great room, kitchen, hearth and breakfast area make the Plainview a sun lover's dream. The covered deck on the back of the house and a covered veranda on the front provide an open view with plenty of fresh air.

A. Sierra

#44M-2745   Price Code 20

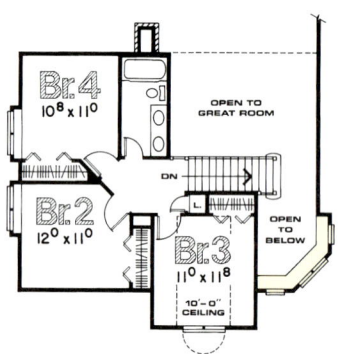

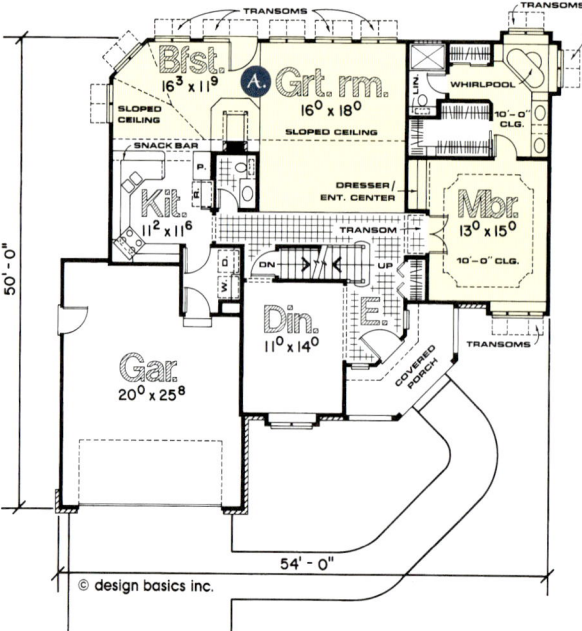

Main: 1510 Sq. Ft.
Second: 579 Sq. Ft.
Total: 2089 Sq. Ft.

IMPRESSIONS— *Homes & Places for Real People*

B. Newberry

#44M-1455   Price Code 25

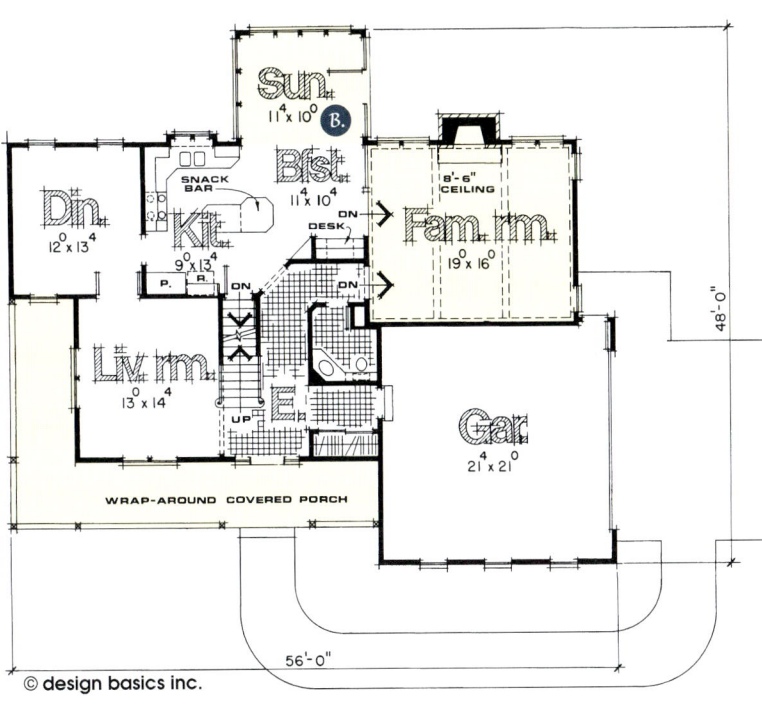

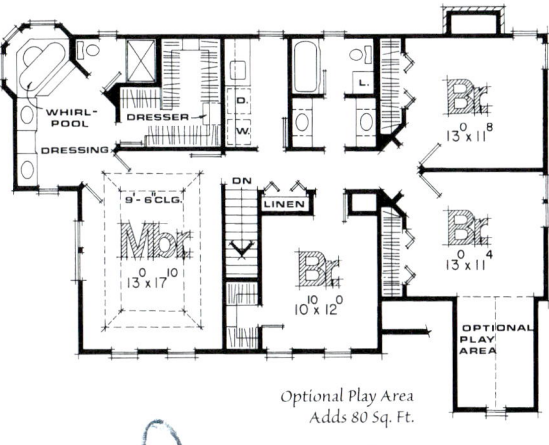

Optional Play Area Adds 80 Sq. Ft.

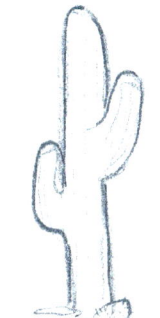

Main: 1322 Sq. Ft.
Second: 1272 Sq. Ft.

Total: 2594 Sq. Ft.

ORDER DIRECT - (800) 947-7526   www.designbasics.com   65

C. Plainview

#44M-2222 Price Code 20

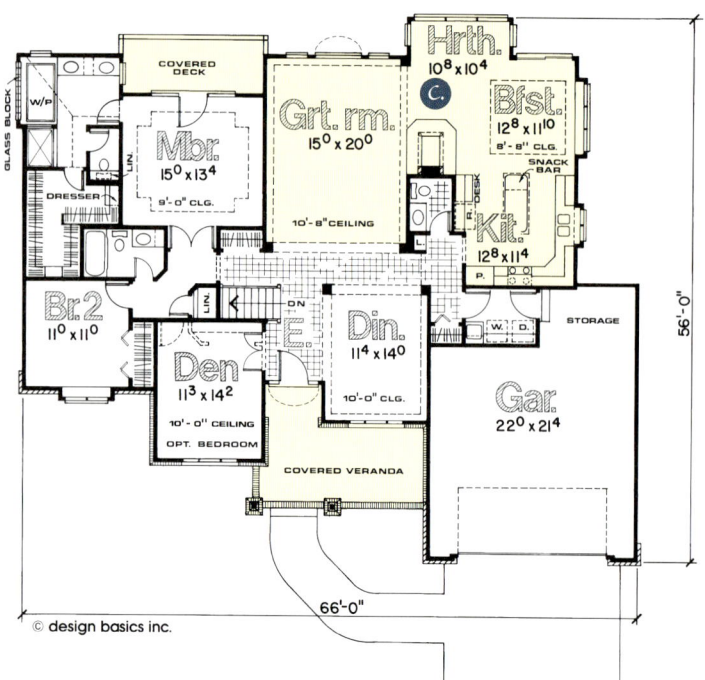

2068 Finished Sq. Ft.

This home may have been altered from the plan's original design.

#44M-3058 *Price Code 23*

Montgomery

This home may have been altered from the plan's original design.

BUILT BY: Timberlake Development

Tyndale

#44M-2245 *Price Code 16*

BUILT BY: Mesenburg Custom Homes
PHOTO BY: Kelly Mesenburg

A half wall brings some definition to the breakfast area, yet continues the open connection with the great room.

An 11-foot-high ceiling in the master bath is given further impact with a large skylight above the whirlpool tub.

A corner walk-in pantry and island kitchen benefit the cook.

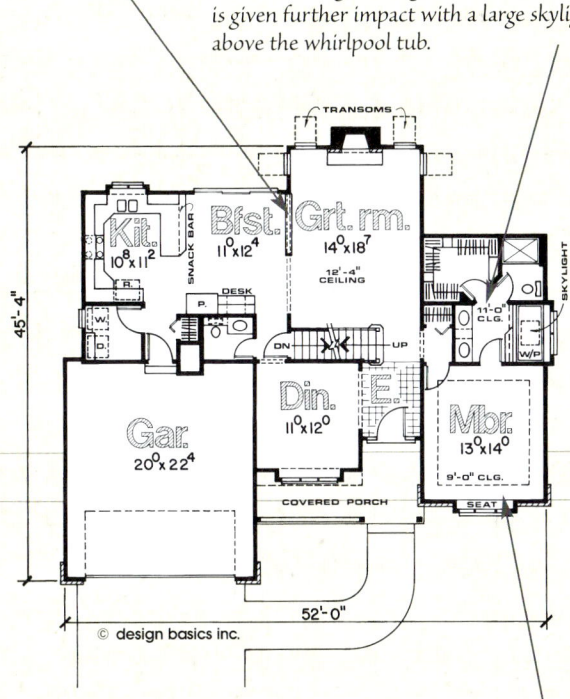

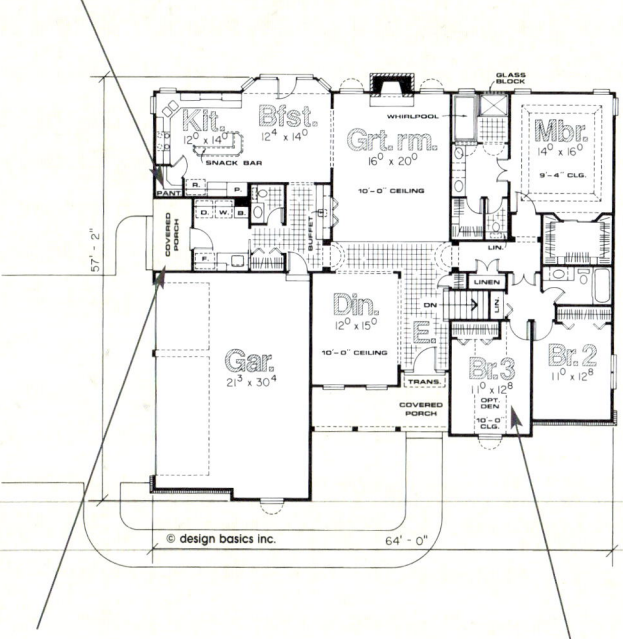

The side covered porch allows one to relax while doing laundry.

Another lovely aspect to the master suite is its built-in window seat—a great spot for reading.

Bedroom 3 easily works as a home office.

Main: 1297 sq. ft.
Second: 388 sq. ft.
Total: 1685 sq. ft.

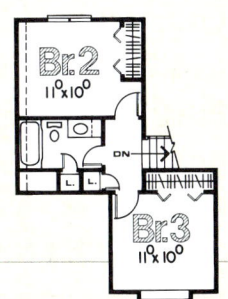

2311 Finished Sq. Ft.

ORDER DIRECT— (800) 947-7526 www.designbasics.com   67

THE NORTHWEST

The kind of scenes found in high quality calendars: A rushing waterfall in a mossy, emerald rain forest. A lonely lighthouse on a rugged coast. Snow-capped mountains floating atop a misty fog. A monochromatic skyline veiled in haze. Douglas firs as tall as trees in fairy tales. Harbors filled with fishing boats. Migrating whales. Salmon swimming upstream. Crimson-covered cranberry bogs. Japanese gardens, flower farms, and meadows in blankets of wild flowers.

Where colorful totem poles tell native family histories... cowboys straddle logs instead of bulls... world famous apples grow everywhere and plaid shirts abound... Nike shoes and Boeing airplanes are produced and Bill Gates started a software empire. A land filled with ethnic pride and colorful festivals.

Those who live in skyscraper forests carry umbrellas at all times, wear unpretentious footwear, ride taxis on water, drink steaming lattes in quaint coffee bars and shop in open air markets where fresh fish fly through the air. They never drop in unannounced or ask a new acquaintance what he does for a living. Although they're naturally reserved and self-effacing, they have a reputation for being hip. Their symphony, theater, ballet and fine cuisine are well respected. But they're best known for starting their own trends with alternative music groups like Pearl Jam and Nirvana.

When the weekend comes, they leave the bustle behind and head outdoors to dig for clams, pick wild mushrooms, ski, scuba dive, hike, hunt, fish, ride horses, climb mountains and kayak down white water rivers. They also go camping, but they always bring a deck of cards along– just in case.

IMPRESSIONS- *Homes & Places for Real People*

Design Quality #9

A. The Sinclair
B. The Hanna
C. The Ellison

Northwestern Solitude...

With today's hectic lifestyles, home often becomes a retreat from the noisy hustle and bustle: A place to renew one's tired spirit. These three homes provide special spots of refuge – quiet spaces to curl up with a good book; fill out a crossword puzzle; catch up on correspondence; or dream dreams for the future and set goals to make them happen.

3 Views...

A. Separated on the opposite end of the house from the other bedrooms, the Sinclair's master suite enjoys complete privacy. With its own entertainment center, the hearth room allows family members to choose their own activities apart from whatever is going on in the great room. The bedroom adjacent to the great room can also be converted into a private den.

B. Those who like to withdraw to their own space from time to time will appreciate the Hanna. It features a master suite on a level all by itself and a computer loft with a built-in desk which overlooks the great room. With a triple-wide window and built in bookshelves, bedroom 2 could also be used as a study.

C. The Ellison offers several spots for quiet getaways: a covered porch with a built-in bench at the rear of the home, a master suite secluded on the main floor and a very private den adjoining the master bedroom.

BUILT BY: Wegher, Peterson, Schultzen Inc.

A. Sinclair

#44M-1748 *Price Code* 19

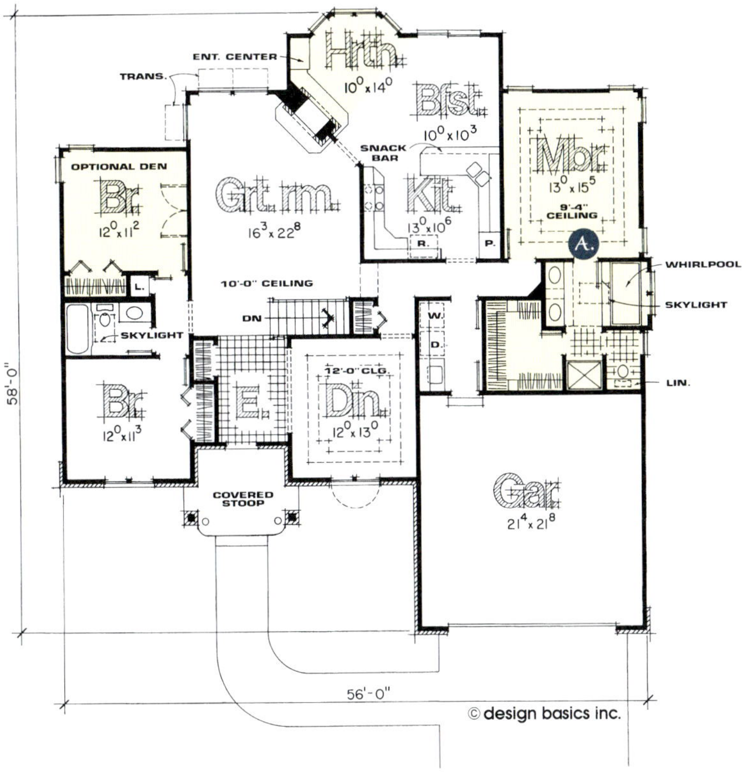

1911 Finished Sq. Ft.

ORDER DIRECT – (800) 947-7526 www.designbasics.com

69

BUILT BY: Cadillac Construction
PHOTO BY: Bestrom Enterprises, LLC.

B. Hanna

#44M-4081 *Price Code 25*

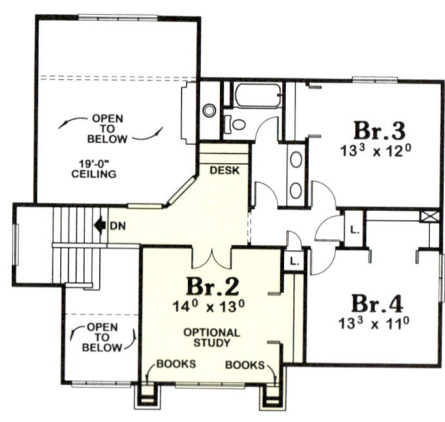

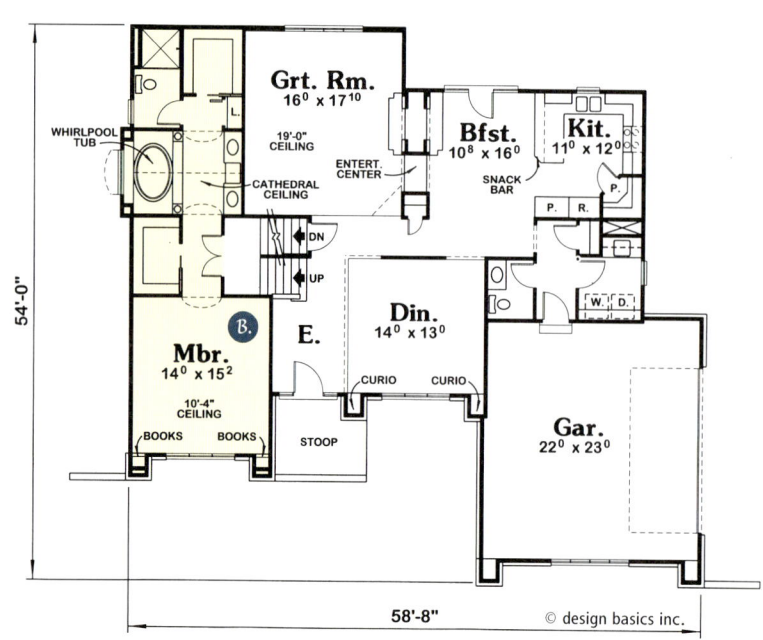

Main: 1735 Sq. Ft.
Second: 841 Sq. Ft.

Total: 2576 Sq. Ft.

NOTE: 9 ft. main level walls

IMPRESSIONS— *Homes & Places for Real People*

BUILT BY: Jerry Hermiller

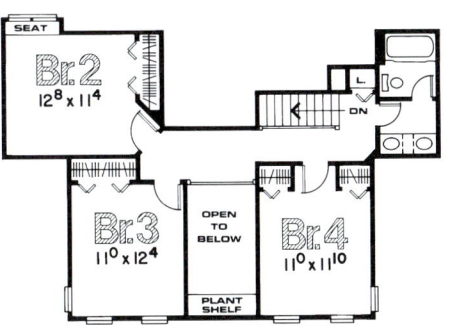

C. Ellison

#44M-2702 Price Code 24

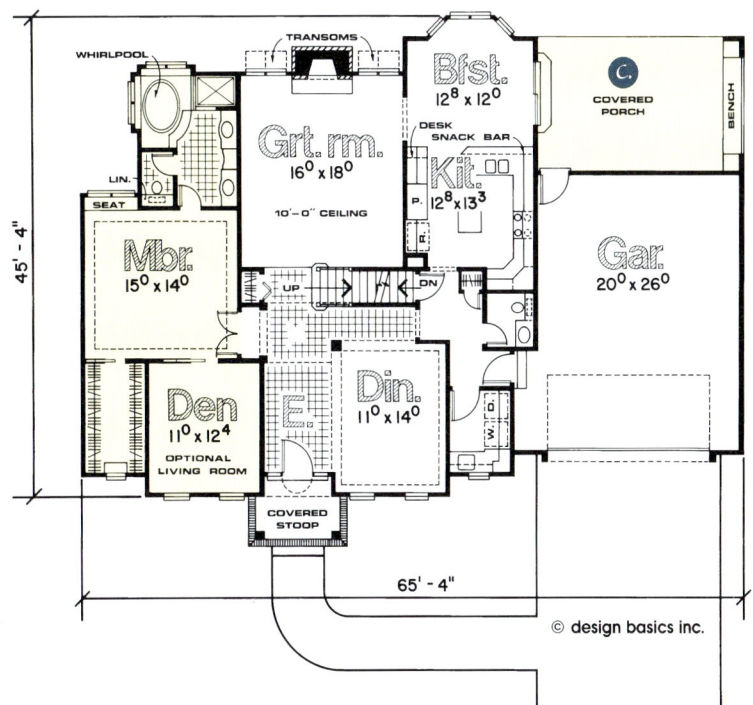

Main: 1716 SQ. FT.
Second: 716 SQ. FT.

Total: 2432 SQ. FT.

ORDER DIRECT - (800) 947-7526 www.designbasics.com 71

Home owner impressions

on living in the Concorde

BUILT BY: Johnston Enterprise Inc.

A busy career couple, Kurt and Christina make the most of living in Washington state by spending lots of time outdoors. They both water and snow ski, golf, scuba dive, and go 4-wheeling.

Their home, Design Basics' "Concorde," also makes the most of their location. The back of the house has plenty of windows to provide a beautiful, panoramic view of the Olympic mountains and the bay. And in what seems to be a bonus, the three-car garage gives its owners ample room for their two cars, a jeep and all of their recreational equipment.

Kurt and Christina discovered the Concorde in a round-about way. They were planning to have a friend build a house for them. He suggested they look at a couple of spec houses he was building to get some ideas. When they toured his Concorde, they fell in love with its spacious kitchen and master bath and its wide, open floor plan.

"The kitchen is beautiful," Kurt explains. It has lots of cabinet space, tile countertops, a hardwood floor and dark cherry cabinets. But the bathroom was probably the biggest turn on, with its big tub and standup shower with dual heads. And it's all tiled; it has tile floors, a tile shower, and tile around the tub."

Another appealing feature is the covered deck on the back of the home. The plan calls for a covered patio, but their home is built on a hill giving them a deck and a

continued on page 74

Concorde

#44M-3597 Price Code 21

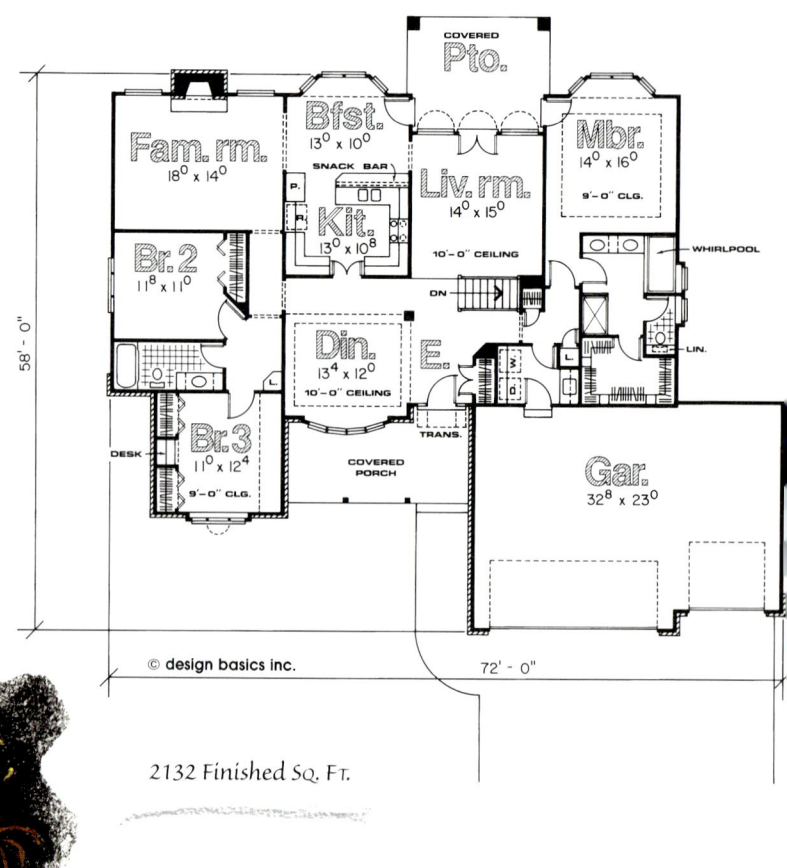

2132 Finished Sq. Ft.

IMPRESSIONS— *Homes & Places for Real People*

BUILT BY: Brewer Construction

Bardel

#44M-24004 *Price Code 22*

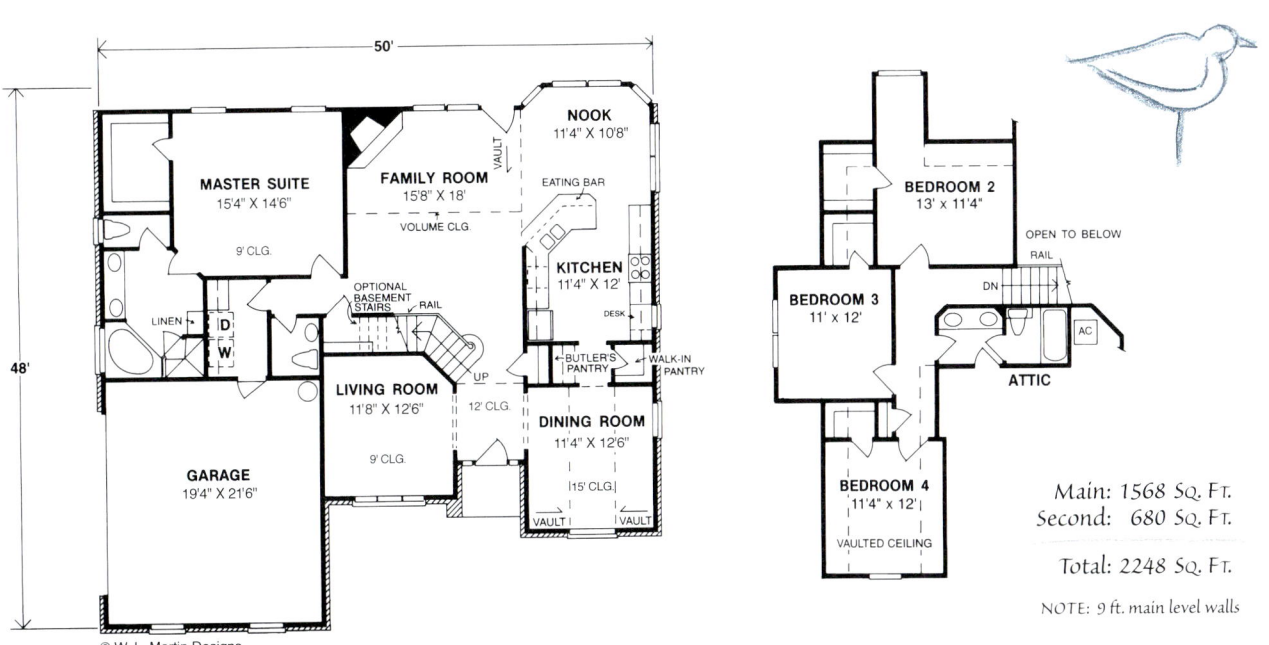

Main: 1568 SQ. FT.
Second: 680 SQ. FT.

Total: 2248 SQ. FT.

NOTE: 9 ft. main level walls

© W. L. Martin Designs

ORDER DIRECT - (800) 947-7526   www.designbasics.com

daylight basement. The couple entertained friends on the 4th of July; they sat on the deck and watched the fireworks down in the bay.

Kurt praises his builder for adding nice touches to the home. "All of the corners are rounded," Kurt comments, "and he made the ceilings different throughout the house. He stepped the ceiling down three levels in the formal dining room and entry way. In the master bedroom, he stepped the ceiling down in an octagon shape. The master bath's ceiling is angled with a nice skylight. Another bedroom showcases yet another type of ceiling. As added touches, the opening into the formal dining room was built as a squared-off arch and light marble outlines a beautiful gas fireplace in the family room."

The home's setting typifies the scenic Northwest. Although the neighborhood is new, it boasts lush landscaping complete with a lovely array of rhododendrons. The area is outlined by woods filled with cedar, alder and evergreen trees and the Olympic mountains rise majestically behind the waterfront town.

Kurt puts in long hours as a used car sales manager, yet he finds time to beautify his own yard. He has put rock walls in the front and back and plans to add a cement pad with a jacuzzi along one of the walls in the back.

The couple has plenty of plans for the inside of their home as well. Their living space doubled when they moved into the Concorde, so they're in the process of looking for additional furniture. They're also looking forward to finishing their daylight basement. It's wide open now, but has plumbing set up for another kitchen and another bathroom. With nearly 2,000 extra square feet downstairs, Kurt and Christina will have room to grow for many years to come.

Manning

#44M- 2207   *Price Code* 29

Main: 1583 SQ. FT.
Second: 1331 SQ. FT.
Total: 2914 SQ. FT.

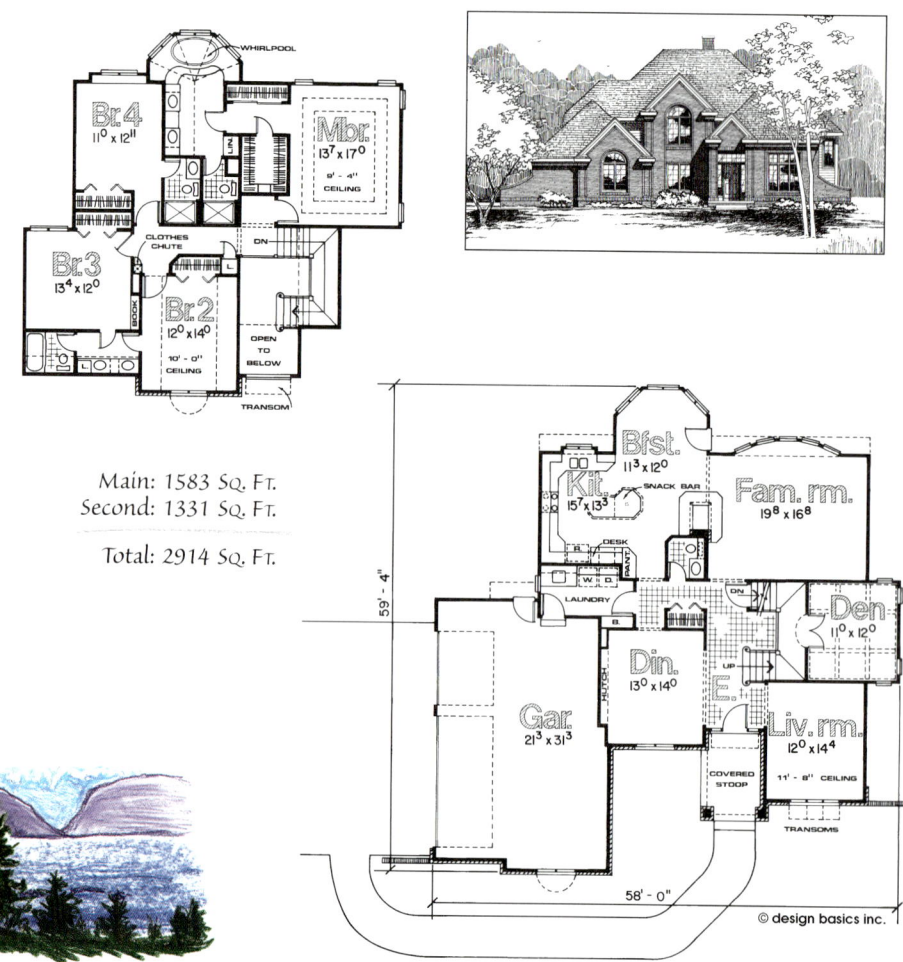

74

IMPRESSIONS- *Homes & Places for Real People*

Paterson

#44M-1380   Price Code 19

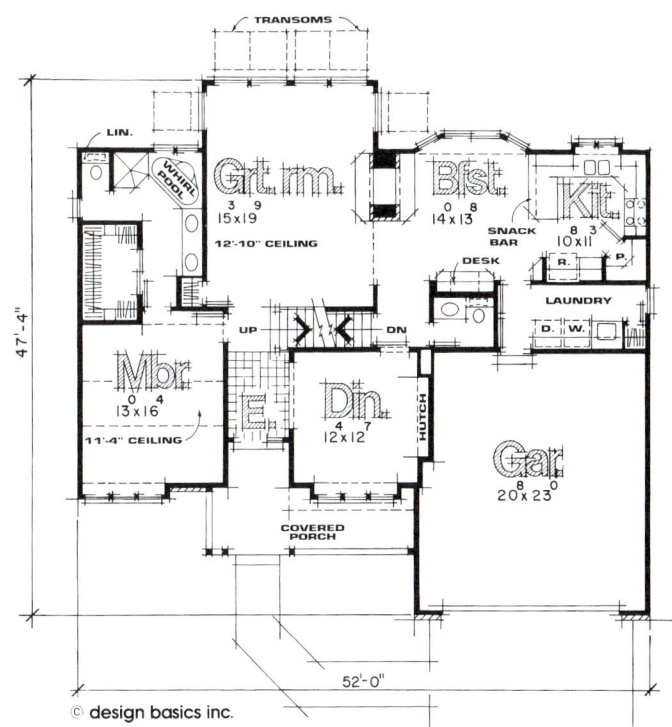
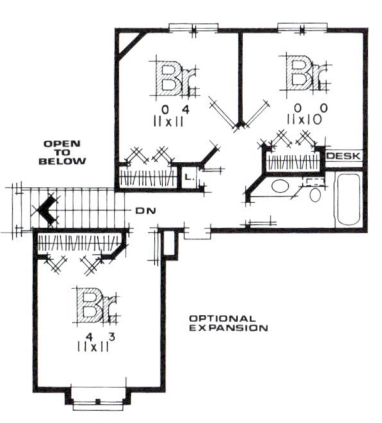

Main: 1421 Sq. Ft.
Second: 578 Sq. Ft.

Total: 1999 Sq. Ft.

This home may have been altered from the plan's original design.

BUILT BY: Muehling Homes

#44M-4134 *Price Code* 26

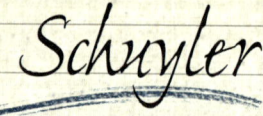

BUILT BY: Ken Oster Homes

Paige

#44M-3581 *Price Code* 17

This home may have been altered from the plan's original design.

Abundant counter space in the kitchen leaves plenty of room for appliances.

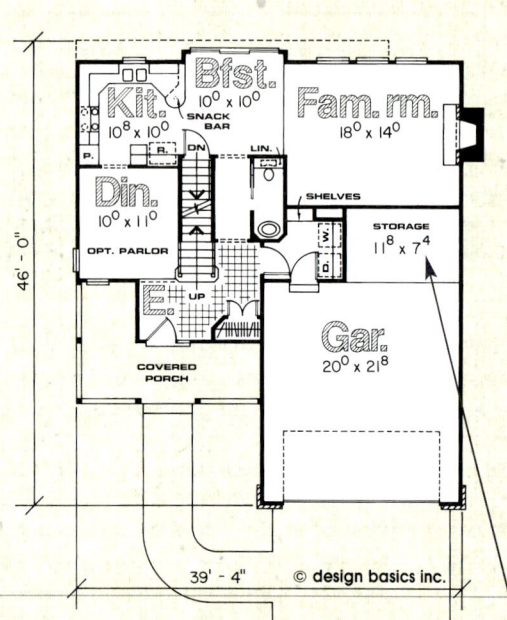

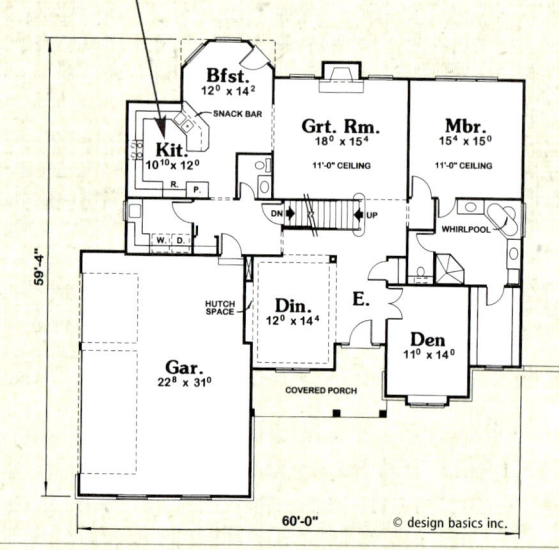

Bicycles, large toys or lawn equipment are easily kept in a roomy storage space in the garage.

Unfinished storage space offers the potential for a hobby or exercise area.

Finishing off an optional toy closet in lieu of a two-story entry could provide needed storage space for a growing family.

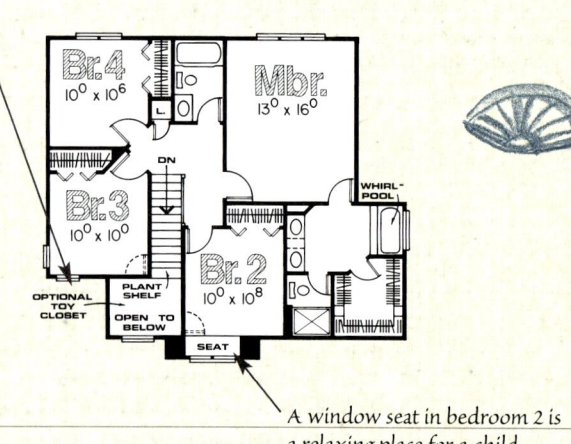

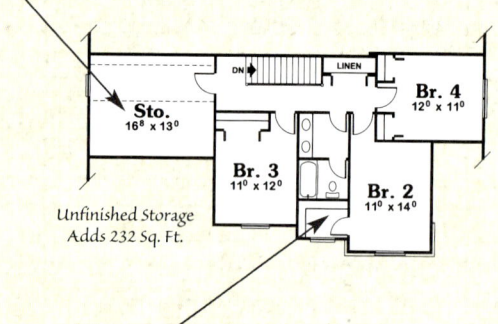

Unfinished Storage Adds 232 Sq. Ft.

A walk-in closet adds extra storage space in bedroom 2.

A window seat in bedroom 2 is a relaxing place for a child.

Main: 866 Sq. Ft.
Second: 905 Sq. Ft.
Total: 1771 Sq. Ft.

Main: 1847 Sq. Ft.
Second: 766 Sq. Ft.
Total: 2613 Sq. Ft.

This home may have been altered from the plan's original design.

BUILT BY: Mycka Custom Homes

Charleston

#44M-3587 *Price Code* 17

#44M-8013 *Price Code* 13

This home may have been altered from the plan's original design.

BUILT BY: Jacobs Construction

Gabriel Bay

This home caters to a casual lifestyle, demonstrated in the open kitchen and hearth room with built-in shelves and cabinetry for home electronic equipment.

A rear screened porch is another great area to entertain guests.

A triple window brightens the master suite highlighting a walk-in closet, corner soaking tub and dual-sink vanity.

L-shaped counters define a walk-thru kitchen with easy access to the laundry room and garage.

A rear view is enhanced with tall windows on either side of a fireplace in the great room.

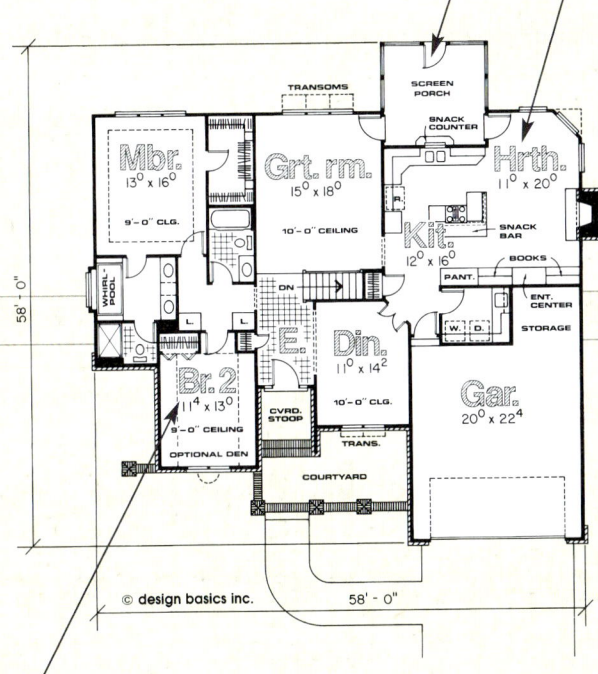

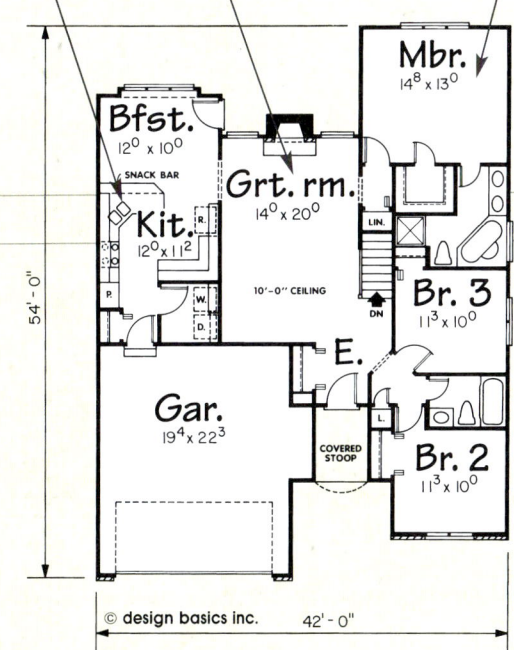

Bedroom 2 could easily be used as a den or home office.

1796 Finished Sq. Ft.

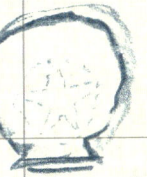

1392 Finished Sq. Ft.

ORDER DIRECT — (800) 947-7526 www.designbasics.com   77

This home may have been altered from the plan's original design.

BUILT BY: Blake Homes

Hamilton Farm

#44M-8072 *Price Code 20*

This home may have been altered from the plan's original design.

BUILT BY: Rockland Homes

Gerard

#44M-4135 *Price Code 23*

A wet bar in the family room is convenient when entertaining formally or informally.

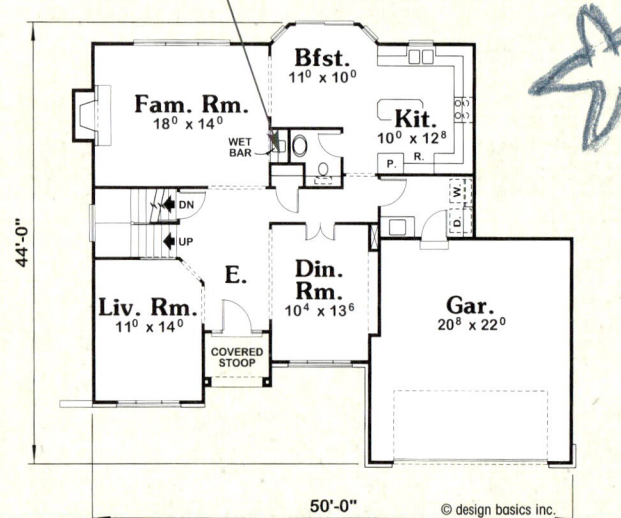

An extra long counter, a nice-sized pantry and an island add convenience to this kitchen.

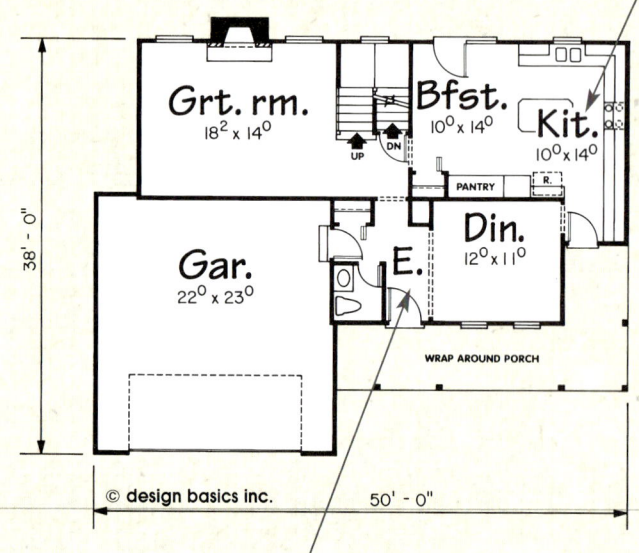

Bedroom 2 with its own private bath makes the perfect guest bedroom or in-law suite.

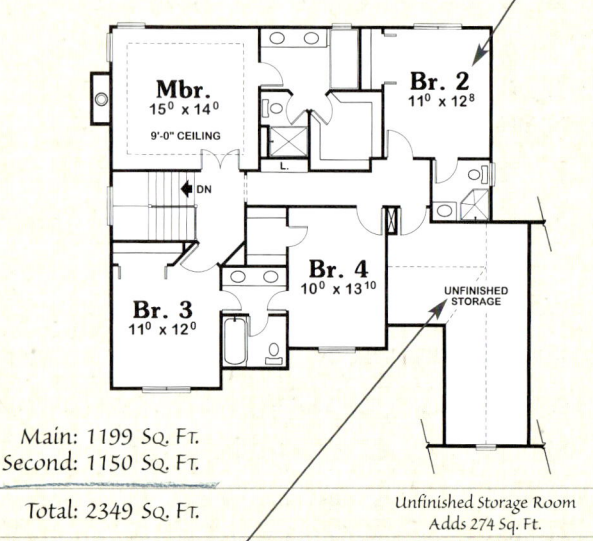

The front entry and a door off the kitchen both lead to the lovely, wrap around porch.

The master bedroom features a dual vanity, compartmented bath and a large, walk-in closet.

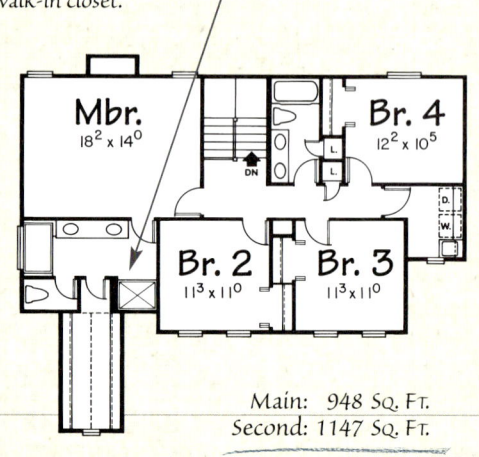

Main: 1199 Sq. Ft.
Second: 1150 Sq. Ft.

Total: 2349 Sq. Ft.

Unfinished Storage Room Adds 274 Sq. Ft.

Unfinished space above the garage provides welcome additional storage to the second floor.

Main: 948 Sq. Ft.
Second: 1147 Sq. Ft.

Total: 2095 Sq. Ft.

IMPRESSIONS - *Homes & Places for Real People*

This home may have been altered from the plan's original design.

BUILT BY: Oehlberg Construction

Rothschild

#44M-2374 *Price Code 28*

#44M-8095 *Price Code 16*

This home may have been altered from the plan's original design.

Sun Valley

BUILT BY: Jacobs Construction

Sunny, bayed kitchen/breakfast area has wet bar/servery and walk-in pantry.

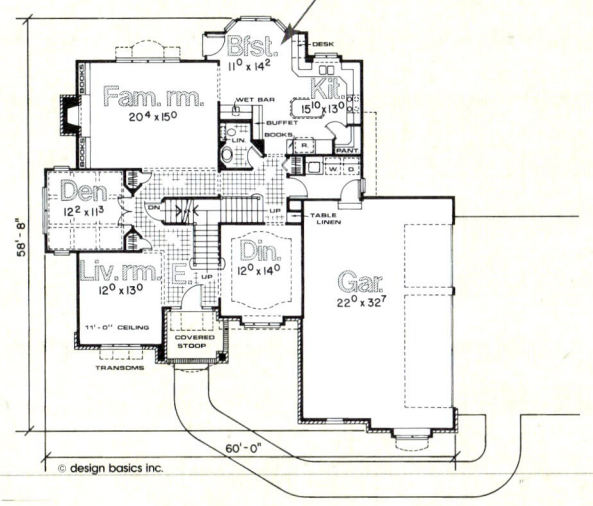

Master suite has vaulted ceiling, his/her vanity, corner whirlpool, separate make-up area and huge, walk-in closet.

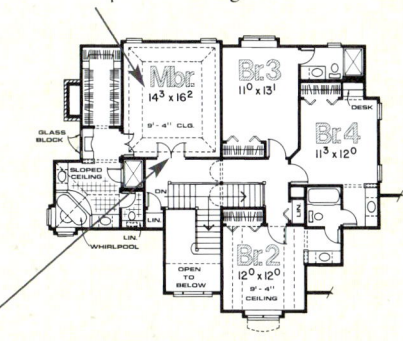

Two-story entry gives dramatic view of French doors to master suite above.

Main: 1575 Sq. Ft.
Second: 1295 Sq. Ft.
Total: 2870 Sq. Ft.

A large snack bar in the kitchen allows one to enjoy a meal or snack while conversing with those in the kitchen.

The tall, transom windows in the great room not only allow an extended view to the back, they also bring in needed light to fill the expanse of the room.

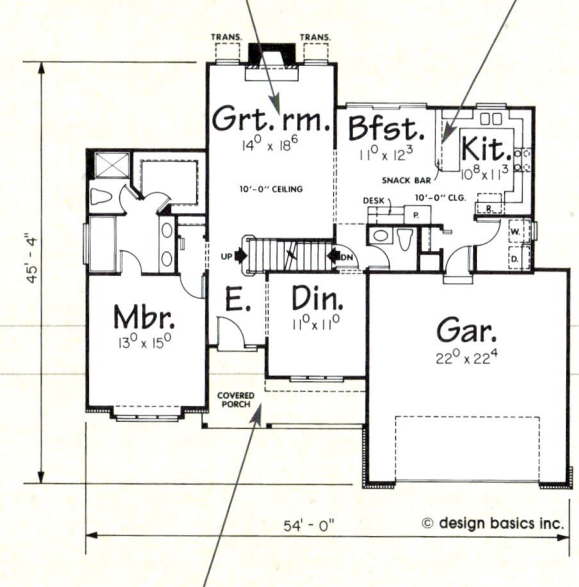

On this home, the front porch is the ideal element to draw visitors into the entry.

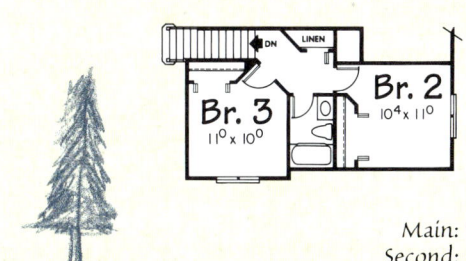

Main: 1298 Sq. Ft.
Second: 396 Sq. Ft.
Total: 1694 Sq. Ft.

ORDER DIRECT- (800) 947-7526 www.designbasics.com

Design Quality #10

A. The Summerwood
B. The Manchester
C. The Jones Farm

Cozy Warmth...

From the beginning of time, homes have been built to provide shelter from the outside world. To keep the rain and the cold winds out. But of course, home is also an emotional shelter. A safe place to hang our hearts. Where we're truly understood because we're free to let our guards down. Where people love us just as we are and believe in us so much we become better. These cozy floor plans embody the warm welcome you love to come home to.

3 Views...

A. A sunny, gazebo-shaped hearth room in the Summerwood is the perfect spot to sip hot chocolate and work on a giant puzzle. The window seat in bedroom 2 is a great place to cuddle up with a quilt and a good novel.

B. Arched windows, a covered porch and gingerbread trim combine to give the Manchester a sense of coziness. A see-thru fireplace in the hearth room spreads an inviting glow throughout the kitchen and breakfast area. Special ceiling treatments in the master bedroom, great room, dining room and breakfast area add ambiance.

C. The country cottage look of the Jones Farm kindles warm feelings as soon as you stop in the driveway. The wrapped porch invites you to rock away an afternoon. Inside, bayed windows in the great room and breakfast areas add a homey touch.

BUILT BY: BCB Enterprises

A. Summerwood

#44M-2361 Price Code 20

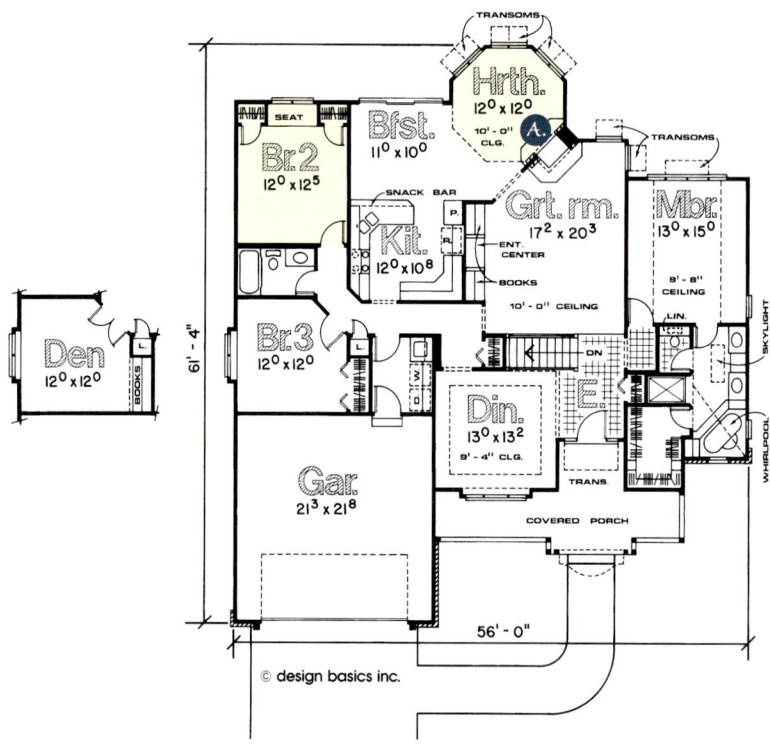

2015 Finished Sq. Ft.

IMPRESSIONS— *Homes & Places for Real People*

BUILT BY: Lapos Construction

B. Manchester

#44M-1862 *Price Code 23*

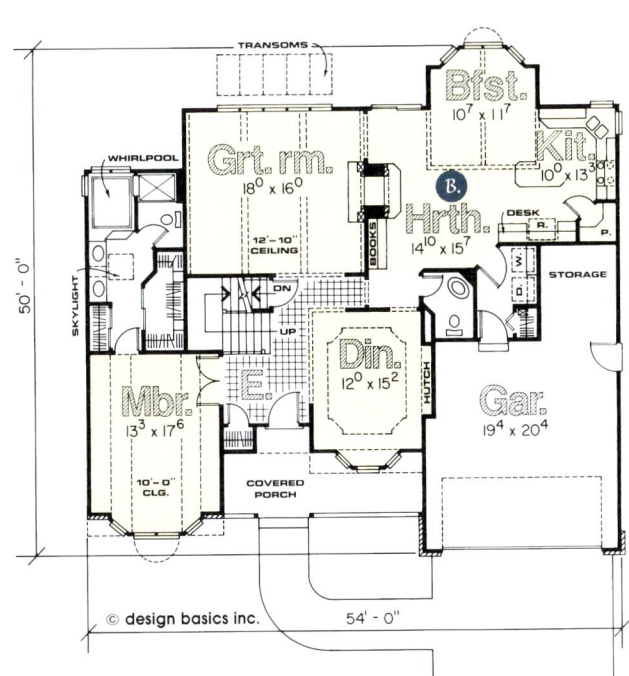
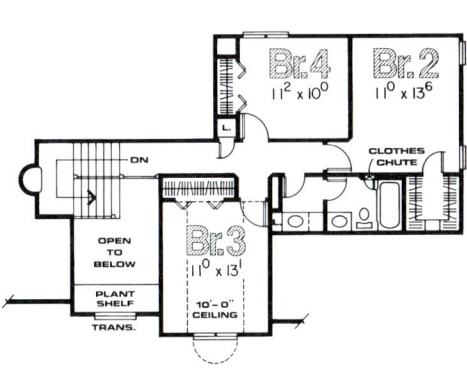

Main: 1653 SQ. FT.
Second: 700 SQ. FT.

Total: 2353 SQ. FT.

BUILT BY: Gemstone Homes

C. Jones Farm

#44M-8011 *Price Code 22*

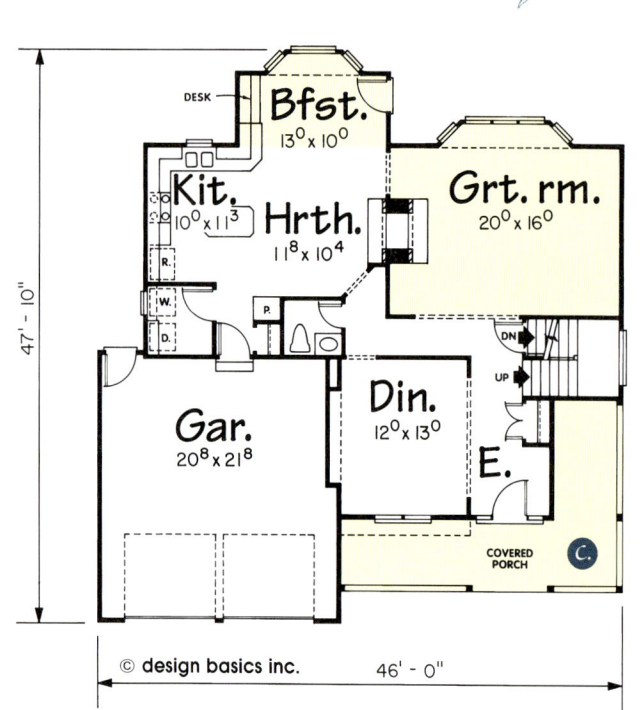

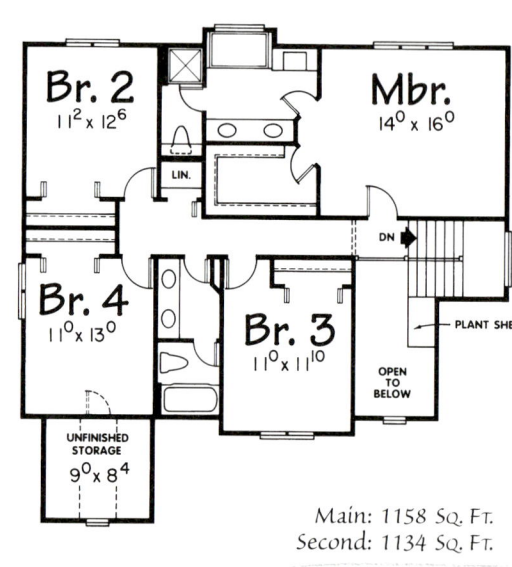

Main: 1158 SQ. FT.
Second: 1134 SQ. FT.

Unfinished Future Room
Adds 84 Sq. Ft.

Total: 2292 SQ. FT.

82

IMPRESSIONS— *Homes & Places for Real People*

This home may have been altered from the plan's original design.

#44M-3578 Price Code 15

Stonybrook

This home may have been altered from the plan's original design.

BUILT BY: Jeff Junkert Construction Inc.
PHOTO BY: Phil Bell

Marlow

#44M-4144 Price Code 30

BUILT BY: Sievers Homes

Certainly one of the most enjoyable aspects of this home will be the kitchen, equipped with a walk-in pantry, double oven, island cooktop and large snack bar.

A fireplace is a relaxing component to the den, great room and hearth room.

The kitchen, breakfast area and bayed hearth room were designed to integrate daily activity with convenience.

Guests will be easily accommodated in the great room with angled, see-thru fireplace and views to the backyard.

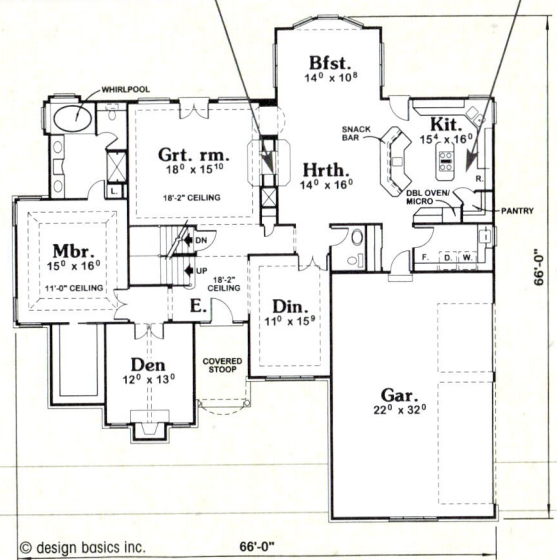

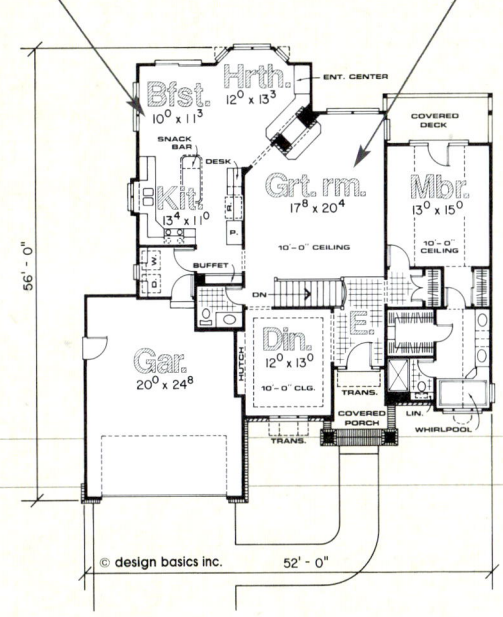

Whether used for storage or as a play room off bedroom 3, this bonus room will be a welcome feature.

1595 Finished Sq. Ft.

Optional Finished Basement Plan Included Adds 790 Sq. Ft.

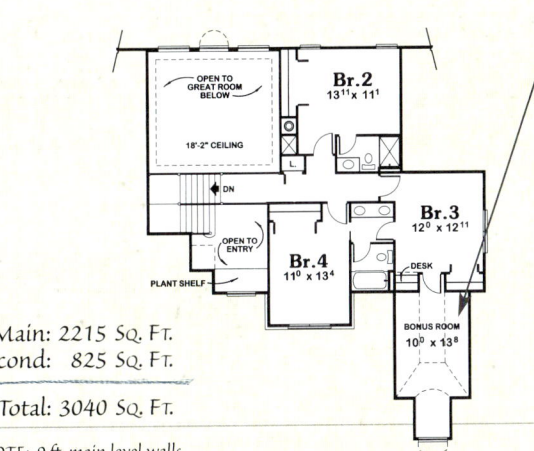

Main: 2215 Sq. Ft.
Second: 825 Sq. Ft.

Total: 3040 Sq. Ft.

NOTE: 9 ft. main level walls

Unfinished Future Room
Adds 186 Sq. Ft.

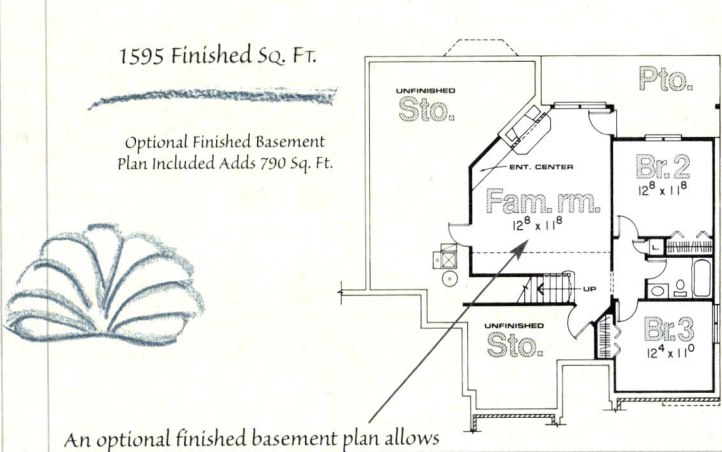

An optional finished basement plan allows this home to grow with a young family.

ORDER DIRECT— (800) 947-7526 www.designbasics.com

83

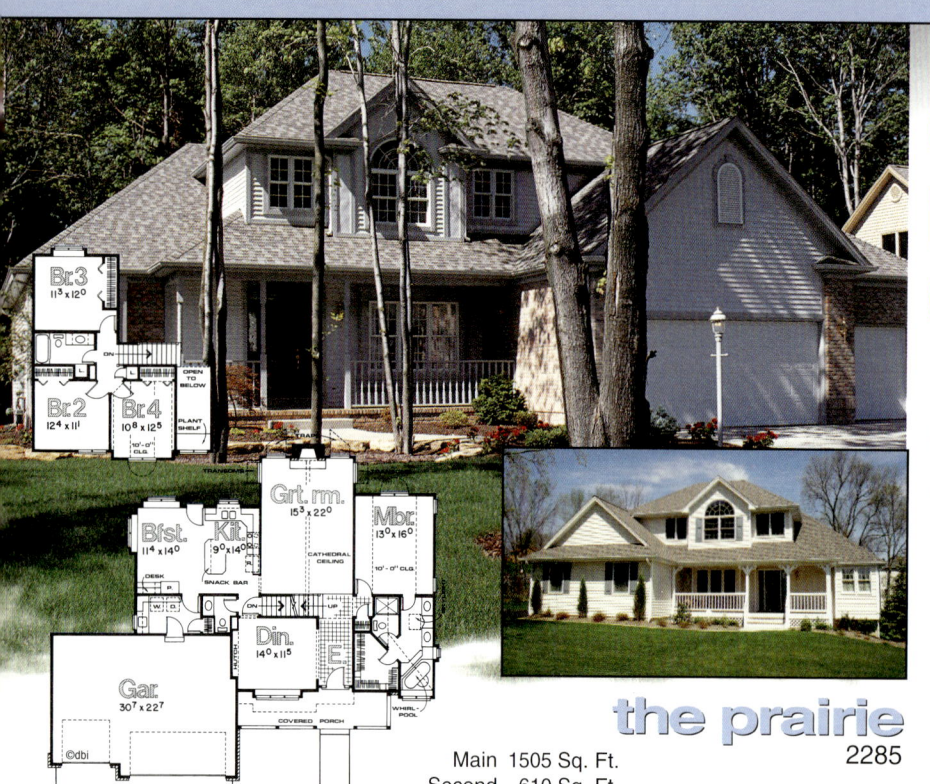

CHANGE IS A GOOD THING

One Floor Plan, Two Different Home.

the prairie
2285

Main 1505 Sq. Ft.
Second 610 Sq. Ft.
Total 2115 Sq. Ft.
Width 64'-0"
Depth 52'-0"

design basics inc
HOME PLAN DESIGN SERVICE

800-947-7526
www.designbasics.com

customchanges

Experience the *feeling of* Home

Neighborhoods — HOME PLAN PORTFOLIO
Hometown — HOME PLAN PORTFOLIO

Both Collections for only $10
plus shipping & handling
While Supplies Last

design basics inc
HOME PLAN DESIGN SERVICE

800-947-7526

WWW.DESIGNBASICS.COM
OVER 1,100 AWARD-WINNING HOME PLANS

Enhance Your Design Basics Experienc
With a Complete Line of Support Materials

Specifications & Finishing
Checklist
Track each selection you need to make...from doorknobs to siding. Only $15.

Material & Estimator's
Workbook
Compare bids and eliminate budgeting errors. Only $50.

Foundations
Choose additional foundations for your plan. Only $75.

Study Print & Furniture
Layout Guide
See what your new rooms will look like furnished. Only $50.

800-947-7526
www.designbasics.com

DESIGN BASICS' HOME PLAN LIBRARY

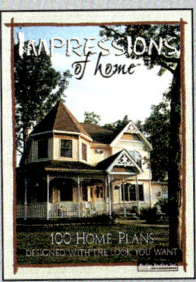
Impressions of Home™ Homes Designed with the Look You Want – 100 home plans from 1339' to 4139'. $4.95

Impressions of Home™ Homes Designed for the Way You Live – 100 home plans from 1191' to 4228'. $4.95

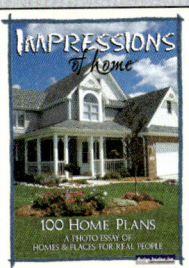
Impressions of Home™ Homes & Places for Real People – 100 home plans from 1341' to 4139'. $4.95

Study of Home™ - Special Places - 100 home plans from 1212' to 3914'. $4.95

Study of Home™ How Home Has Changed - 100 home plans from 1212' to 4500'. $4.95

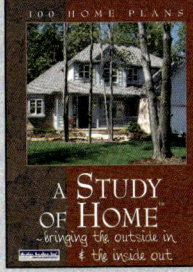
Study of Home™ Bringing the Outside In - 100 home plans from 1212' to 4500'. $4.95

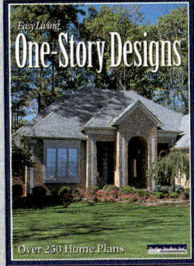
Easy Living One-Story Designs™ 252 home plans from 962' to 3734'. $7.95

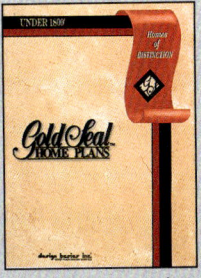
Gold Seal™ Home Plan Book Set - All 5 books for $50.00 or $10.00 each **Homes of Distinction** - 86 plans under 1800'

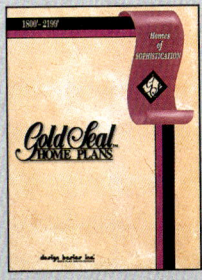
Gold Seal™ Home Plan Book Set - All 5 books for $50.00 or $10.00 each **Homes of Sophistication** - 106 plans, 1800'-2199'

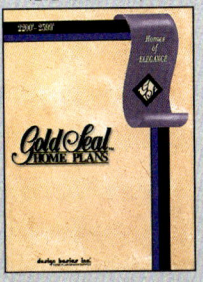
Gold Seal™ Home Plan Book Set - All 5 books for $50.00 or $10.00 each **Homes of Elegance** - 107 plans, 2200'-2599'

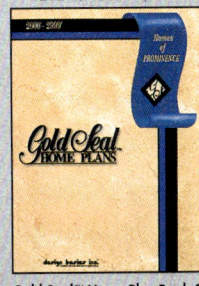
Gold Seal™ Home Plan Book Set - All 5 books for $50.00 or $10.00 each **Homes of Prominence** - 75 plans, 2600'-2999'

Gold Seal™ Home Plan Book Set - All 5 books for $50.00 or $10.00 each **Homes of Grandeur** - 68 plans, 3000'-4000'

Nostalgia Home Plans Collection™ A New Approach to Time-Honored Design - 70 home plans from 1339' to 3480'. $9.95

Nostalgia Home Plans Collection™ Vol. II - A New Approach to Time-Honored Design 70 home plans from 1191' to 3858'. $9.95

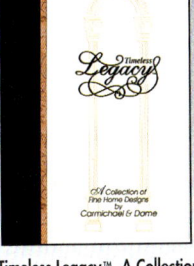
Timeless Legacy™, A Collection of Fine Home Designs by Carmichael & Dame – 52 home plans from 3300' to 4500'. $15.00

The Homes of Carmichael & Dame™ Vol. II 60 home plans from 1751' to 4228'. $9.95

W.L. Martin Home Designs 53 home plans from 1262' to 3914'. $9.95

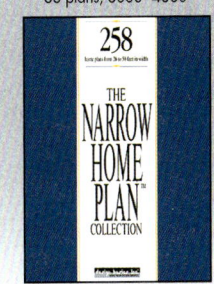
The Narrow Home Plan™ Collection 258 home plans from 962' to 2517'. $14.95

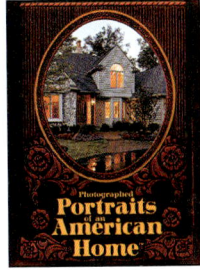
Photographed Portraits of an American Home™ 100 home plans from 1205' to 4228'. $14.95

Reflections of an American Home™ Vol. III 50 home plans from 1341' to 3775'. $4.95

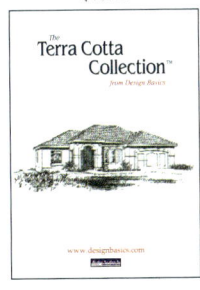
The Terra Cotta Collection™ 9 Southwestern Style Home Plans from 1528' to 2716'. $3.00

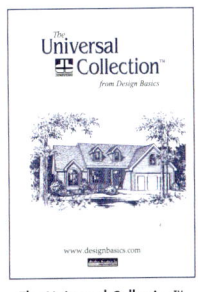
The Universal Collection™ 15 ADA Home Plans from 1394' to 2785'. $3.00

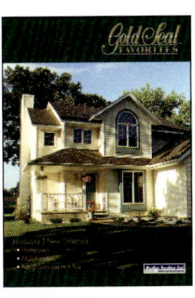
Gold Seal Favorites™ – 144 plans from the Gold Seal, Hometown, Multi-Family and Neighborhood in a Box Collections. 1125' to 5420'. $6.95

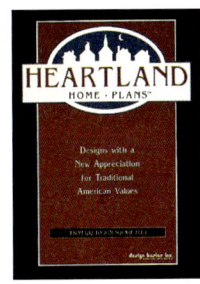
Heartland Home Plans™ 120 home plans from 1212' to 2631'. $8.95

Simply Plans™ 115 Home Plans from 1205' to 4139'. $4.95

Simply Plans™ Vol. II 118 Home Plans from 1190' to 4500'. $4.95

Neighborhoods™ 78 Home Plans from 1195' to 2705'. $7.00

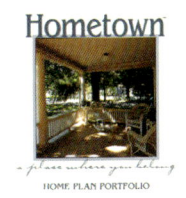
Hometown™ 26 Home Plans from 1190' to 1590'. $3.00

(800) 947~7526

www.designbasics.com

What Do I Get With a Design Basics Plan?

CONSTRUCTION LICENSE

When you purchase a Design Basics home plan, you receive a Construction License which gives you certain rights in building the home depicted in that plan, including:

No Re-Use Fee. As the original purchaser of a Design Basics home plan, the Construction License permits you to build the plan as many times as you like.

Local Modifications. The Construction License allows you to make modifications to your Design Basics plans. We offer a complete custom change service, or you may have the desired changes done locally by a qualified draftsman, designer, architect or engineer.

Running Blueprints. Your plans are sent to you on vellum paper that reproduces well on your blueprint machine. The Construction License authorizes you or your blueprint facility, at your direction, to make as many copies of the plan from the vellum masters as you need for construction purposes.

CONSTRUCTION DRAWINGS

1. **Cover Page.** Each Design Basics home plan features the rendered elevation and informative reference sections including: general notes and design criteria;* abbreviations; and symbols for your plan.
2. **Elevations.** Drafted at 1/4" scale for the front and 1/8" scale for the rear and sides. All elevations are detailed and an aerial view of the roof is provided, showing all framing members.
3. **Foundations.** Drafted at 1/4" scale. Block foundations and basements are standard. We also show the HVAC equipment, structural information,* steel beam and pole locations and the direction and spacing of the floor system above.
4. **Main Level Floor Plan.** Drafted at 1/4" scale. Fully dimensioned from stud to stud for ease of framing. 2"x4" walls are standard. The detailed drawings include such things as structural header locations, framing layout and kitchen layout.
5. **Second Level Floor Plan.** Drafted at 1/4" scale. Dimensioned from stud to stud and drafted to the same degree of detail as the main level floor plan.*
6. **Interior Elevations.** Useful for the cabinet and bidding process, this page shows all kitchen and bathroom cabinets as well as any other cabinet elevations.
7. **Electrical and Sections.** Illustrated on a separate page for clarity, the electrical plan shows suggested electrical layout for the foundation, main and second level floor plans. Typical wall, cantilever, stair, brick and fireplace sections are provided to further explain construction of these areas.

Full Technical Support is available for any plan purchase from Design Basics. Our Technical Support Specialists provide unlimited technical support free of charge and answer questions regarding construction methods, framing techniques and more. Please call 800-947-7526 for more information.

* Design Basics plans are drafted to meet average conditions and codes in the state of Nebraska, at the time they are designed. Because codes and requirements can change and may vary from jurisdiction to jurisdiction, Design Basics Inc. cannot warrant compliance with any specific code or regulation. All Design Basics plans can be adapted to your local building codes and requirements. It is the responsibility of the purchaser and/or builder of each plan to see that the structure is built in strict compliance with all governing municipal codes (city, county, state and federal).

COPYRIGHT Cans & Cannots

These days it seems almost everybody has a question about what can or can-not be done with copyrighted home plans. At Design Basics, we know U.S. copyright law can sometimes get complex and confusing, but here are a few of the basic points of the law you'll want to remember.

Once you've purchased a plan from us and have received a Design Basics construction license:

You Can...
- Construct the plan as originally designed, or change it to meet your specific needs.
- Build it as many times as you wish *without* additional re-use fees.
- Make duplicate blueprint copies as needed for construction.

You Cannot...
- Build our plans without a Design Basics construction license.
- Copy *any* part of our original designs to create another design of your own.
- Claim copyright on changes you make to our plans.
- Give a plan to someone else for construction purposes.
- Sell the plan.

PROTECT YOUR RIGHTS to build, modify and reproduce our home plans with a Design Basics construction license.

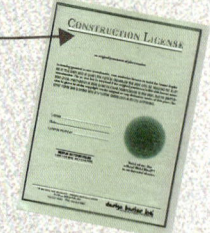

The above points are provided as general guidelines only. Additional information is provided with each home plan purchase, or is available upon request at (800) 947-7526.

PLAN PRICE SCHEDULE

PLAN CODE	TOTAL SQ. FT.	PRICE
9	900' - 999'	$575
10	1000' - 1099'	$585
11	1100' - 1199'	$595
12	1200' - 1299'	$605
13	1300' - 1399'	$615
14	1400' - 1499'	$625
15	1500' - 1599'	$635
16	1600' - 1699'	$645
17	1700' - 1799'	$655
18	1800' - 1899'	$665
19	1900' - 1999'	$675
20	2000' - 2099'	$685
21	2100' - 2199'	$695
22	2200' - 2299'	$705
23	2300' - 2399'	$715
24	2400' - 2499'	$725
25	2500' - 2599'	$735
26	2600' - 2699'	$745
27	2700' - 2799'	$755
28	2800' - 2899'	$765
29	2900' - 2999'	$775
30	3000' - 3099'	$785
31	3100' - 3199'	$795
32	3200' - 3299'	$805
33	3300' - 3399'	$815
34	3400' - 3499'	$825
35	3500' - 3599'	$835
36	3600' - 3699'	$845
37	3700' - 3799'	$855
38	3800' - 3899'	$865
39	3900' - 3999'	$875
40	4000' - 4099'	$885
41	4100' - 4199'	$895
42	4200' - 4299'	$905
43	4300' - 4399'	$915
44	4400' - 4499'	$925
45	4500' - 4599'	$935
46	4600' - 4699'	$945
47	4700' - 4799'	$955
48	4800' - 4899'	$965
49	4900' - 4999'	$975
2X	Duplex	$845
3X	Tri-Plex	$945
4X	4-Plex	$1045

PRICES SUBJECT TO CHANGE